TAX SURVIVAL for CANADIANS

Stand Up to the CRA

Dale Barrett, Tax Lawyer

Self-Counsel Press
(a division of)
International Self-Counsel Press Ltd.
Canada USA

Self-Counsel Press acknowledges the financial support of the Government of Canada through the Canada Book Fund for our publishing activities.

First edition: 2013

Printed in Canada.

Library and Archives Canada Cataloguing in Publication

Barrett, Dale, 1974-
    Tax survival for Canadians: stand up to the CRA / Dale Barrett.

Issued also in electronic format.
ISBN 978-1-77040-039-9

    1. Tax auditing–Canada–Popular works. 2. Canada Revenue Agency–Popular works. 3. Law for laypersons. I. Title.

KE5705.B37 2013	343.7104	C2012-901791-4
KF6314.B37 2013		

Self-Counsel Press
(a division of)
International Self-Counsel Press Ltd.

Bellingham, WA	North Vancouver, BC
USA	Canada

CONTENTS

6 What to Expect If You Are Audited

10 Interest and Penalty Relief   83

11 CRA Collections   93

15 Tax Schemes

16 First Nations Taxation

17 When You Need a Little Help

Conclusion

Samples

Tables

NOTICE TO READERS

Laws are constantly changing. Every effort is made to keep this publication as current as possible. However, the author, the publisher, and the vendor of this book make no representations or warranties regarding the outcome or the use to which the information in this book is put and are not assuming any liability for any claims, losses, or damages arising out of the use of this book. The reader should not rely on the author or the publisher of this book for any professional advice. Please be sure that you have the most recent edition.

This book provides general information only, and can point you in the right direction and provide things for you to consider in your dealings with the Canada Revenue Agency, but it should not be relied on by any means as a substitute for personalized, solid, and professional advice from a tax lawyer.

Note: The fees quoted in this book are correct at the date of publication. However, fees are subject to change without notice. For current fees, please check with the court registry or appropriate government office nearest you.

Prices, commissions, fees, and other costs mentioned in the text or shown in samples in this book probably do not reflect real costs where you live. Inflation and other factors, including geography, can cause the costs you might encounter to be much higher or even much lower than those we show. The dollar amounts shown are simply intended as representative examples.

DEDICATION

To my beautiful wife, Nicole, and my entire family who have patiently been along side me throughout all the craziness of my career fighting to make the Canadian tax system a little more fair for the taxpayers.

Thanks for everything … I know that at times, dealing with me has been very taxing.

INTRODUCTION

For those who follow the tax golden rule: If a taxpayer always files his or her tax returns honestly, perfectly, and on time, keeps all supporting documentation, and pays all his or her taxes when due, the person need not fear the Canada Revenue Agency.

For all others: Beware.

Canada's tax laws are very powerful and the way in which these laws are applied may have very serious consequences for a taxpayer. The outcome is sometimes fair, and sometimes not. And due to the great power bestowed upon the Canada Revenue Agency (CRA), there is a great possibility that tax laws can be used to oppress taxpayers.

Lord Denning, a famous and influential English judge, said of tax legislation that it is "… drawn so widely that in some hands it might be an instrument of oppression. It might be said that: honest people need not fear: that it will never be used against them … that is an attractive argument, but I would reject it. Once great power is granted, there is a danger of it being abused."

Recently I spoke to a taxpayer who, like many other Canadians, operated a small corporation with three employees who worked with the owner and his wife. The corporation performed oil field consulting services in the oil sands of Northern Alberta for 15 years. The corporation had a tax debt of approximately $200,000 and with its current contracts it would have been able to pay the entire debt off within a year or less. Unfortunately for the corporation, its three employees, and its husband and wife owners, the cry for help came too late. By the time I provided a preliminary consultation, the corporation was in the midst of closing down.

Despite the fact that the corporation had been generating a profit of more than $25,000 per month after all employees and expenses were paid, and would have easily and quickly been able to pay off its tax bill, a number of things had gone wrong. The tax debt had been accumulating over a number of years, but the corporation was able to weather and survive various recessions which had caused many other businesses in the oil industry to fail. With the sharp rise in oil prices, the corporation was finally gaining strength and over the year prior to my consultation with the taxpayer, the corporation had been able to reduce its tax debt from $425,000 to less than half of that; however, this was not good enough for the Canada Revenue Agency (CRA). The CRA wanted the debt paid off in full and the collections agent would not wait any longer.

Within a one-week period, the director of the corporation had discovered that the corporate bank account was frozen, and that all remaining funds had been taken by the CRA. Further, he learned that the CRA would be giving him 30 days in which to pay off the debt in full. Unfortunately because the corporation was in trouble with the CRA, the banks would not lend any funds to pay off the debt, and the director of the corporation was forced to comply with a number of harsh demands made by the CRA in order to arrange a payment plan for the outstanding debt and to have its bank account unfrozen.

These demands included providing bank statements and credit card statements for the three previous months as well as financial records, an accounts receivable listing, and the names of all corporate clients. The taxpayer was told that this information had to be provided in order to prove to the CRA that the corporation could afford the $20,000 per month payment plan that had been proposed by the director. The collections agent promised that the information from the taxpayer would only be used to verify income and determine ability to pay, and the taxpayer thought it would be best to fully comply with the request. By co-operating with the CRA, the taxpayer provided information which was ultimately used against the corporation.

By the time I had spoken to the taxpayer, the CRA had already send a letter to each of the corporation's five clients advising them that if they owed any money to the corporation that they were required by law to remit it to the CRA instead of to the corporation. This effectively blocked any payments to the corporation from its clients.

Within days of being provided with the client list, the CRA had effectively stopped the flow of all funds to the corporation, leaving it without the means to pay employees or purchase fuel for its trucks. Further, these letters damaged the corporation's reputation severely within the industry, and out of fear that the corporation could no longer deliver services effectively, four of its five contracts were cancelled within days. By the time the CRA had released the corporate bank account, there was no more business to be had, there were no employees left to fulfill the remaining contract, and there was a husband and wife team who had already remortgaged their home in order to help their business during the rough times.

Within a few weeks the couple started missing mortgage and vehicle payments, and within a few short months they lost their home and one of their two vehicles, and had to sell virtually everything they owned in order to survive.

The corporation was forced to shut down, and since the tax debt was primarily GST and payroll source deductions, as directors of the corporation, the couple was faced with the director's liability claims causing a brand new collections agent at the CRA to pursue them personally for the debt.

Ultimately after the corporation closed, the taxpayers obtained employment working for companies in their industry. But after they were personally assessed for the corporation's debt, and after their wages were garnished by 40 percent to pay the CRA, they had no choice but to declare personal bankruptcy and end the torment.

At the end of the day, following the freezing and emptying of the corporate bank account, which resulted in approximately $13,000 of the tax debt being paid, and following the closure of the corporation, the loss of five jobs, and the personal bankruptcies of the two directors, the CRA never received another dime of the $200,000 in outstanding taxes, which otherwise would have been paid within the year.

This is not a unique story. This happens every day in every province and territory across Canada.

In order to understand the CRA, you must familiarize yourself with the structure of the CRA, the mechanics of filing taxes, and the complexities of dealing with the CRA's employees. Without understanding the basics, many of which are outlined in this book, you should not expect to succeed in defending yourself against the CRA. However, understanding the basic mechanics of the CRA is not enough. What

most people do not realize, and why many people find it frustrating to deal with the CRA, is that in order to really understand it, you must realize that while it is governed by laws and rules, it is run by people and their personalities which are not always consistent or fair.

To understand the CRA is to understand how its employees operate. Despite how logical you think you are, and despite how much faith you have in the Canadian government, if you have not dealt with the many hundreds of collections agents within the CRA, you will have virtually no chance at predicting what they will do next or how they are motivated. This is because they don't operate the way collections agents in the real world operate. They do not receive a commission for taxes collected, and thus by and large, do not really care if the tax debt is actually collected by the CRA. Instead, a great many collections agents are more concerned with closing a file quickly than they are concerned with collecting the debt — even if it means forcing a taxpayer into bankruptcy.

To be able to understand the CRA employees, and in order to effectively deal with the agency — especially the collections agents — you must leave traditional logic behind. You need to get into the mindset of the public servant on the other end of the phone who perhaps aspires to be a manager one day, and wants a pay increase each year, but wants to go home at 4:30 when his or her shift is over.

You must think about what it is like to work for a company that has a virtually unlimited budget and will always have the money to pay its employees regardless of how much money the employees earn for it or how the economy is doing. Consider what it is like to work for a company that always has money for its payroll and a company that could never go bankrupt or close down. It's a company where employees can make whatever promises they want to the clients, but invariably refuse to put anything in writing so they can routinely break those promises and not suffer any consequences. Consider it a company that rewards employees for closing files rather than earning money, and allocates more money towards the employees' budget for each conviction of taxpayers in criminal court for failing to file a return on time. In essence, it is a company that is so very different from any company in the country that its employees have lost touch with how a real business operates. When you understand all of this, you will begin to understand the CRA.

1
INTRODUCING THE
CANADA REVENUE AGENCY (CRA)

Section 91(3) of the *Constitution Act*, 1867, provides the ability for the federal government to tax, and section 92(2) provides that ability for the provinces to tax. It was not until 1917 that the federal government started to apply an income tax, which was imposed to help finance World War I. At the time of the war, more than 90 percent of tax revenues were from indirect taxes; a number which has decreased sharply over the years. Today, income tax provides the greatest component of taxes collected by the government, and it has never disappeared from the Canadian landscape.

The Canada Revenue Agency (CRA) is a federal agency responsible for administering the tax laws of Canada such as the *Income Tax Act* and the *Excise Tax Act*, as well as the laws of many provinces and Aboriginal governments.

Formed pursuant to the *Canada Revenue Agency Act*, the CRA is the backbone of taxation in Canada, without which nobody would file returns or pay taxes and the entire country would grind to a halt. Our airports and borders would stop operating. Our soldiers wouldn't be paid to protect our country, and the police wouldn't be paid to patrol our cities. In short, the CRA is a necessity, and in order to achieve its mandate of administering the taxation system, it has been given very broad powers to get the job done.

Besides the administration of the domestic tax system, the CRA is the body that is involved with the administration of tax agreements between Canada and various other countries. It also administers various types of social benefits and incentive systems such as the Canada Pension Plan and Employment Insurance, and it oversees the registration of Canadian charities.

1. Your Relationship with the CRA

Taxpayers have a complicated relationship with the CRA. When it comes time to pay their taxes, taxpayers are not too pleased with the CRA; however, when taxpayers receive benefits or tax refunds, attitudes quickly change for the better. The relationship is complicated by the fact that there are certain obligations that taxpayers have towards the CRA, which they may not always wish to respect, and in turn there are certain rights that taxpayers have when dealing with the CRA — rights the CRA routinely overlooks and violates.

1.1 Your rights

Some of the taxpayers' rights come from statutes such as the Canadian Charter of Rights and Freedoms and the *Income Tax Act*. Certain other rights come directly from the Taxpayer Bill of Rights.

Put forth in 2007, the Taxpayer Bill of Rights includes a series of 15 rights that in theory (and not always in practice) are supposed to be guaranteed to each taxpayer. Some of these come directly from statute, such as the right to relief from interest and penalties that arise due to extraordinary circumstances, while other rights, such as the right to expect the CRA to be accountable, are service-related rights, complaints about which are overseen by the Taxpayers' Ombudsman.

According to the Taxpayer Bill of Rights poster available from the CRA, you have the right —

- to receive entitlements and to pay no more and no less than what is required by law;
- to service in both official languages;
- to privacy and confidentiality;
- to a formal review and a subsequent appeal;
- to be treated professionally, courteously, and fairly;
- to complete, accurate, clear, and timely information;
- as an individual, not to pay income tax amounts in dispute before you have had an impartial review;
- to have the law applied consistently;
- to lodge a service complaint and to be provided with an explanation of the CRA's findings;
- to have the costs of compliance taken into account when administering tax legislation;
- to expect the CRA to be accountable;
- to relief from penalties and interest under tax legislation because of extraordinary circumstances;
- to expect the CRA to publish its service standards and report annually;
- to expect the CRA to warn you about questionable tax schemes in a timely manner; and
- to be represented by a person of your choice.

1.2 Your obligations

Simply put, the obligations of a Canadian taxpayer are to respect tax legislation and do all the things required by such legislation and by the CRA in the time frame required. This means that taxpayers must file returns and pay their taxes when required to do so, and cooperate with the CRA's requests for information during the course of an audit or investigation, unless the investigation is criminal in nature, in which case the taxpayers may avail themselves of the Canadian Charter of Rights and Freedoms against self-incrimination and unreasonable search and seizure.

As long as Canadian taxpayers honestly and diligently discharge their duties to the CRA (which includes keeping all documents for the CRA if that time comes), they usually have nothing to fear. However, if a taxpayer runs into trouble, or has a fire that destroys his or her documents, he or she may be in for a rough ride — regardless of how honest and diligent he or she has been.

2. What the CRA Knows about You

The CRA knows a great deal about taxpayers because it keeps extensive and detailed records. Like a giant computerized elephant, the CRA does not forget recorded taxpayer information, and as its databases and computer systems become more sophisticated over time, it is better able to use this information to its benefit — often to the taxpayers' detriment.

A taxpayer must trust that the CRA will use every piece of information at its disposal against a taxpayer. When it comes time to freezing a taxpayer's bank account, the CRA remembers each payment made and the financial institution from which the cheque was drawn; when it comes time to granting (or denying) a request for taxpayer relief, the CRA will be able to point to that time 20 years in the past where the taxpayer was late on filing his or her return by a day, and will use this delinquency as a basis to deny relief which theoretically is guaranteed as a right.

Some personal information that the CRA has in its database comes directly from taxpayers. Every time you file an income tax return with the CRA, the information from your returns becomes part of the permanent record.

If you are audited, the CRA learns more about you and adds this information to its database. If you speak to the collections officers, they take detailed notes which are also added to your record. The CRA knows when you have made payments, the promises you have broken, and the financial institution you use to pay your taxes.

The CRA also obtains information passively from a taxpayer's employer. For example, whenever an employer provides a taxpayer with a T4 slip, the employer also sends that information to the CRA. So whether or not you have filed your tax return, the odds are that the CRA knows how much income you have earned.

Through information requests and periodic checks of taxpayer credit reports, the CRA can obtain a whole host of additional information about a taxpayer, his or her assets, and his or her financial transactions from employers, clients, financial institutions, accountants, and other third parties. All the information that the CRA has obtained, whether passively or actively, will be used to ensure that it has extracted the right amount of taxes from a taxpayer.

While the CRA is fairly diligent in its information collection and processing, in some cases, the CRA has incorrect information about a taxpayer, and in the course of an audit or an objection to a reassessment, the taxpayer may be put in the position where he or she has to use his or her own documentation to prove the CRA is wrong. When reassessments or assumptions of the CRA auditors are incorrect, a taxpayer's ability to produce correct documentation can greatly impact his or her financial future, and in the case of a business, its success or failure. As such, it is imperative that both individuals and business owners are in the position to properly dispute incorrect reassessments by producing the necessary documentation.

According to item one of the Taxpayer Bill of Rights, taxpayers have the right to receive entitlements and pay no more and no less than required by law. However, if the CRA has the wrong information, and attempts to assess taxpayers for more than is required by law, taxpayers must be ready to challenge the CRA's interpretation and application of the facts and law to ensure that they are not paying more than their fair share. This is the burden of the taxpayers, and once the CRA assesses taxes, they are assumed to be correct unless it is proven otherwise. If a taxpayer waits too long to make the challenge, the assessment is set in stone and is not subject to being changed — no matter how incorrect it is.

It must be kept in mind that irrespective of the fact that the CRA is assumed to be correct, notices of reassessment which appear to be incorrect are not necessarily an indication that the taxpayer, or his or her accounting professional, has done something wrong. Often the CRA makes a mistake, which stems from a faulty assumption or incorrect documentation about a taxpayer. In order to uphold a taxpayer's right not to pay more than he or she is required to by law, it is crucial to understand the CRA's system for maintaining information on taxpayers (see section 2.1).

In 2009 and 2010, the CRA audited approximately 380,000 small- and medium-sized businesses and issued notices of reassessment requiring these businesses to pay $2.1 billion in additional tax, interest, and penalties. In many cases, these reassessments could have been challenged, and the tax payable could have been reduced by providing the proper documentation.

While most returns are processed by the CRA without manual review, as to ensure the taxpayer's timely receipt of notices of assessment, it must be kept in mind that every return is in fact screened by the CRA and is susceptible to later review. Amazingly, the processing time is usually between two to six weeks for the 25 million returns filed yearly in Canada.

Practically every tax lawyer who has dealt directly with the CRA will agree that unless dealing with the simplest of issues, resolution is never simple. There are factors that aggravate the complexity of dealing with the CRA, such as understanding the *Income Tax Act* (ITA), a very complex statute, as well as dealing with the CRA. The CRA is comprised of a massive administrative body, which can make it unreasonable for a self-represented taxpayer to expect a simple resolution to his or her tax problems — especially without proper record keeping.

The following sections discuss the types of information the CRA collects about the taxpayers.

2.1 Information slips

Information slips are issued and prepared by payers, employers, and administrators, and are required for Canadian income tax returns to report many types of income, including benefits that one has paid during a tax year. Typically, taxpayers receive three copies of each information slip — one copy must be submitted with their federal tax return, the second copy must be submitted with their provincial or territory tax return, and the third copy must be kept as a record by the taxpayer.

The following are the various types of information slips:

- **T3 — Statement of Trust Income Allocations and Designations:** This slip is issued by trustees and financial administrators to advise the CRA and the taxpayer about earned income for the year from business trusts, estates, and mutual funds in non-registered accounts.

- **T4 — Statement of Remuneration Paid:** This slip is issued by employers to employees to advise the CRA and the taxpayer of employment income the taxpayer earned during a tax year and the amount of income tax that was deducted at the source. Employment income includes bonuses, commissions, salary, tips, vacation pay, taxable allowances, value of taxable benefits, honorariums, and payment in lieu of notice.

- **T4A — Statement of Pension, Retirement, Annuity, and Other Income:** Employers issue this slip to employees to inform the CRA and the taxpayer of earned income from a given tax year, including the amount of income tax deducted. It may further be issued by corporate directors, pension administrators, trustees, or estate executors or liquidators.

- **T4A(OAS) — Statement of Old Age Security:** This slip is issued by Service Canada to advise the CRA and the taxpayer of Old Age Security income earned by the taxpayer during a tax year, including the amount of income tax deducted.

- **T4A(P) — Statement of Canada Pension Plan Benefits:** This slip is issued by Service Canada to advise the CRA and the taxpayer of Canada Pension Plan (CPP) benefits received during a tax year, including the amount of income tax deducted. CPP benefits include child benefits, retirement benefits, death benefits, and survivor benefits.

- **T4E — Statement of Employment Insurance and Other Benefits:** Service Canada issues this slip to advise the CRA and the taxpayer of Employment Insurance benefits paid to the taxpayer for the previous tax year, including any income tax deducted, and any amount paid toward an overpayment.

- **T4RIF — Statement of Income from a Registered Retirement Income Fund:** This slip is issued by financial institutions to advise the CRA and the taxpayer of monies received out of one's Registered Retirement Income Fund (RRIF) for a given tax year and how much tax was deducted.

- **T4RSP — Statement of RRSP Income:** This slip is issued by financial institutions to advise the CRA and the taxpayer of monies withdrawn or received from one's Registered Retirement Savings Plan (RRSP) for a given tax year and how much tax was deducted.

- **T5 — Statement of Investment Income:** This slip is issued by organizations which pay royalties, dividends, or interest, in order to advise the CRA and the taxpayer of investment income earned for a given tax year. Investment income includes insurance policies, interest earned from bank accounts, annuities, bonds, and any account with a broker or investment dealer.

- **T5007 — Statement of Benefits:** Issued by agencies or bodies to report payments for workers' compensation benefits or social assistance.

- **RC210 — Statement of Advance Payments for Working Income Tax Benefit:** This slip is issued by the CRA to advise the taxpayer of any working income tax benefit payments that were made to the taxpayer during the year.

- **RC62 — Statement of Universal Child Care Benefit:** Issued by Human Resources and Skills Development Canada, this slip outlines the total Universal Child Care Benefits paid to the taxpayer during a tax year and any repayment of benefits from a previous year.

2.2 Information arising from "requests" for information

In order to accomplish audit and enforcement activities, the CRA has been provided with broad rights to review taxpayers' books and records. Information is not limited to access of information merely within the taxpayers' possession; so long as it is within the course of conducting the audit or inspection, it is possible that the CRA may seek relevant information in the possession of others.

To that end, the CRA has been provided by law with substantial authority to access all types of documents. This broad authority includes access to documents of third parties, auditors', and accountants' papers that may be relevant to the taxpayer's books and records, or to the enforcement or administration of relevant tax legislation. It is important to note that although this authority is broad, it is still subject to important exceptions, such as the solicitor-client privilege or relevant litigation privilege.

According to the CRA's policy statement (available on the CRA website), the collection of information by officials is done in the least intrusive and most direct manner, but in practice this is not always the case. Oftentimes auditors will attempt to collect information from the source that is most likely to provide it to them the fastest — regardless of any inconvenience, cost, or embarrassment to the taxpayer.

Typically, officials narrow their requests to documents that are within the scope of review, and will generally communicate directly with the taxpayer to retrieve relevant documents or records. Such information is often only sought from third parties when the taxpayer is not or has not been cooperative in providing the information.

2.3 Information from other countries

Canada has agreements with numerous other countries, which prevent the double taxation of income otherwise subject to tax in both countries. These agreements (i.e., tax treaties) contain elaborate rules to determine which country gets to tax the income, and what part of the income the country may tax.

Besides preventing double taxation and establishing a country's turf in terms of ability to tax a given taxpayer, these tax treaties also provide for the exchange of information between treaty partners. At the time of writing, in Canada there are currently 89 tax treaties in force, 10 more which have been signed but are not yet in force, and 2 more under negotiation. What this means for a taxpayer, is that there are potentially 101 countries which can be called upon by the CRA to provide any information it has on the taxpayer's dealings in that country. This includes any financial transactions and records, income, pension earnings, and any other relevant information necessary for the CRA to enforce domestic taxation laws. Any income that one has earned or stashed in these countries is subject to being divulged to the CRA voluntarily, or as a result of a request. Further, some of the treaty countries will even cooperate with the CRA's requests to obtain payment owed by a taxpayer and may seize assets and bank accounts held abroad by the taxpayer.

2.4 Information from financial institutions

To the extent possible, financial information is collected directly from the taxpayer, but in cases where such information is not made available by the taxpayer, rest assured the CRA will obtain it directly from a financial institution. Canadians should take notice that any and all information about a taxpayer that is being held by a financial institution is subject to being obtained by the CRA.

There are absolutely no privacy rights between the taxpayers and their financial institutions. It is of relative ease for the CRA to obtain any financial information it requires from a financial institution.

2.5 Information from tax returns of third parties

The CRA obtains information about taxpayers from information returns filed by third parties with respect to specific transactions. It then compares and verifies the information received by the third parties to ensure the taxpayers have accurately reported on their tax returns. This system of match and detect is frequently used to detect any non-filing of returns. Information returns predominantly deal with —

- partnerships carrying on business in Canada;

- employee paid remuneration;

- corporate security transactions if the corporation deals or trades in securities;

- financial institutions payment of accrued bond interest;

- offshore investments, including foreign affiliates, non-resident trust distributions or transfers, and designated foreign property (e.g., estate, portfolio investments, bank accounts) of Canadians if the total property value exceeds $100,000; and

- interest, dividends, or royalty payments to Canadian residents, and other payments to non-residents of Canada.

2.6 Information gathered from third parties about unnamed taxpayers

Sometimes the CRA launches an investigation into a group of people it doesn't even know the names of yet. It used to be a well-established law that if the CRA wanted information about known taxpayers, it could simply issue a requirement to produce such information and serve it upon those third parties it believed would have the information. However, until recently, the CRA was not investigating groups of unknown people so the law on the matter had not yet developed.

One case that was the focus of a lot of public attention involved the CRA's demands for eBay Canada to produce records and documents relating to Canadian "Power Sellers." The CRA wanted to verify whether these Power Sellers, who have notoriety on eBay for high sales volumes, had reported all of their eBay income on their returns. Based on the decision in a similar case where the CRA had obtained a court order requiring the Greater Montreal Real Estate Board to provide information regarding real estate agent members, eBay ended up providing the information requested.

In the Greater Montreal Real Estate Board case, the CRA initially obtained a court order for a list of the names of all the agent members including a list of properties sold by each. The CRA was investigating what it believed was widespread failure of real estate agents to report all their commissions. Rejecting the challenge mounted by the Real Estate Board, the Federal Court of Appeal noted that section 231.2 of the *Income Tax Act* permitted the CRA to conduct "fishing expeditions" as long as the necessary court orders or warrants were obtained.

2.7 Information gathered from the taxpayer

Information is gathered from the taxpayers at the time of filing, and at the time of any subsequent review of their returns.

Taxpayers are required to file a return if they owe any taxes to the CRA for the relevant reporting period, or if they have been requested to file by the CRA. There are also various other reasons why a taxpayer may be required to file a return, which are discussed in Chapter 3.

If there is no tax payable, and if a taxpayer is not caught by one of these reasons, then no return needs to be filed, and thus the CRA will not gather any information from the taxpayer for that given year — that is unless the CRA performs an audit for that year.

According to section 150(1) of the *Income Tax Act* (ITA), annual tax returns must be filed by taxpayers in the prescribed form, which means providing the CRA with certain data points (i.e., each figure in a tax return is a data point, such as CPP contributions and taxes deducted at source). Filed returns should include documentation to support relevant income and expenses; however, detailed books and records themselves are not to be included with the filing. Section 230 of the ITA explains that although not all information is required to be filed, it is essential that the taxpayer maintain these books and records of accounts in case of later review.

Once the returns have been provided by the taxpayer, and either before or after issuance of the initial Notice of Assessment, the CRA may seek further information regarding the taxpayer's tax obligations. The CRA may simply request additional information or may audit the taxpayer on either a narrow or broad basis. Depending on the type of audit, the auditor may focus narrowly on specific issues, or investigate on more of a large-scale review, auditing all aspects of the taxpayer's finances, including personal and business finances.

3. Confidentiality

When the Minister obtains filed returns or other relevant information, confidentiality prevents the use of this information, unless specifically for the administration and enforcement of the *Income Tax Act* (ITA). Confidentiality of taxpayer information within the income tax collection system in Canada is paramount.

The CRA is prohibited in all but certain specified instances from disclosing taxpayer information, according to section 241 of the ITA. The Supreme Court of Canada, in Slattery (Trustee of) v. Slattery [1993], has commented on the purpose of section 241 as follows:

"Section 241 involves a balancing of competing interests: the privacy interest of the taxpayer with respect to his or her financial information, and interest of the Minister in being allowed to disclose taxpayer information to the extent necessary for the effective administration and enforcement of the *Income Tax Act* and other federal statutes referred to in s 241(4). Access to financial and related information about taxpayers is to be taken seriously, and such information can only be disclosed in prescribed situations. Only in those exceptional situations does the privacy interest give way to the interest of the state."

Section 241 of the ITA limits the scope of confidentiality to taxpayer information only. Taxpayer information includes any type of information, so long as it relates to the taxpayer, that has been created for or by the Minister for the purposes of the ITA or is prepared from such information but does not include information that does not directly or indirectly reveal the identity of the taxpayer to whom it relates.

Essentially, the CRA is prohibited by the ITA from knowingly using taxpayer information for purposes other than for the course of administrative or enforcement under the ITA, including prohibition against knowingly allowing access to or knowingly providing taxpayer information to any person. Agency officials who are in breach of this confidence are subject to penalties under subsection 239(2.2) of the ITA. Penalties may include imprisonment of up to 12 months, and/or fines of up to $5,000.

Moreover, according to subsection 241(2) of the ITA, agency officials cannot be compelled to produce or provide any evidence relating to a taxpayer for use in a non-tax related legal proceeding.

Re Glover v. Glover related to a case in which Mrs. Glover was awarded the custody of her two young children who were then removed from the home by Mr. Glover. In an attempt to track down Mr. Glover, a judge of the Supreme Court of Ontario ordered the CRA to provide the Court with Mr. Glover's address. Upon an appeal of the initial decision, the Court of Appeal of Ontario concluded that Mr. Glover's address was necessary to the CRA and an integral part of the information received by the CRA. Thus according to law, this information could only be provided by the CRA to persons authorized by law to receive it. According to the court, neither the Supreme Court of Ontario nor Mrs. Glover was such a person under section 241, and thus the CRA was prohibited from providing it to them.

Unlike the case in Re Glover v. Glover, a taxpayer's information is not always protected by law. In fact, the Minister is authorized by the ITA to break confidentiality by disclosing taxpayer information in certain instances, such as the administering of criminal justice, government programs, or of the ITA itself. This disclosure occurs when the taxpayer's privacy interest is outweighed by the public interest in administering justice. According to section 241 of the ITA, disclosure of taxpayer information is permitted when related to —

- imminent danger of physical injury or death to any individual,
- criminal proceedings,
- the transfer of information from and between the government, and
- legal proceedings that are related to the administration enforcement of the ITA.

An interesting exception to highlight under subsection 241(3) is in connection to criminal proceedings when commenced by the laying of an "information" (i.e., in order to prosecute, this document provides information about the crime the person is suspected to have committed) or a "charge." In this exception, the CRA cannot initiate the criminal proceeding by using confidential information; the CRA must base its case on independently obtained evidence. Only once an actual charge has been laid, the proceedings initiated, and the need for confidential information to substantiate the case, may confidential information then be used.

For example, this exception would apply when the CRA suspects that a taxpayer may be a drug dealer. In this case the CRA would be prevented from providing information to the police that would result in laying charges for the crime. However, if the police had already charged an individual with this crime, the CRA would be permitted to provide personal information that may assist the Crown in making its case against the taxpayer.

Taxpayers' are not without hope when compelled to disclose confidential tax information in a criminal proceeding. Instances have shown taxpayers successfully stopping disclosure by the CRA by invoking section 11 of the Charter of Human Rights. This is shown in Tyler v. M.N.R. [1991], where the taxpayer was facing charges both criminally and under the *Narcotic Control Act* when the Minister required the taxpayer to hand over confidential tax information, including statements of assets, liabilities, income, and expenses, pursuant to subsection 231.2 of the ITA. Although the information was required by the CRA, it intended to communicate this information to the police while the charges were outstanding. This allowed for the taxpayer to successfully prevent the release of such information, arguing that providing such information would deny him the right to silence under section 11 of the Charter of Human Rights, which says that a person who has been charged of an offence has the right "not to be compelled to be a witness in proceedings against that person in respect of the offence." This would appear to include having to provide information to the CRA which in turn could be incriminating or provide evidence against oneself which could be used in court. In this case, an order was issued by the Federal Court of Appeal to prohibit the CRA from releasing information or communicating with the police regarding the confidential taxpayer information received in the statements.

3.1 Third party confidential information

Competing interests exist with respect to third party confidentiality rights in contrast to the taxpayer's right to access of information from the CRA. There is a strong public policy interest in guaranteeing that taxpayer information remains confidential, hence the balance of these interests often weighs in favor of the taxpayer.

Sometimes, when a taxpayer needs to access the information of another party in order to make his or her case, a balancing test must be performed to see if it is justifiable to release the information of a third party for the benefit of another taxpayer's case.

For instance, in MNR v. Huron Steel Fabricators (London), the trial judge used the balancing test to determine if the public interest would be harmed by the disclosure of tax returns by a company which was not party to the action. The court's decision that no public harm existed withstood appeal. Similar decisions have been found when courts determine that the public interest is best served by production of information.

Other cases have provided additional safeguards for taxpayers by further limiting disclosure, such as in the case of Amp of Canada Ltd. v. The Queen, where the court limited the use of the competitor's materials by imposing restrictions. The court limited the use of the competitor's information only for the period of litigation; the disclosure was only to be made to expert witnesses and counsel; and the materials were to only be used for the purposes of the litigation.

While there have been cases where confidential information has been disclosed to the CRA, the opposite is also true. Take for instance the case of Crestbrook Forest Industries Ltd. v. The Queen; the corporate taxpayer sought from the CRA during a discovery request, the production of specific information that the CRA had relied on in the tax assessment of the corporation. The source from which the CRA had obtained the information was from a survey.

The participants of the survey were told that providing information during the survey was entirely confidential. Hence, it would be contrary to public interest should confidentiality be broken by providing information obtained under the promise of confidentiality. As such, the Federal Court of Appeal prohibited the production of such information. The court explained in this case that, "where the Crown has obtained information in confidence from taxpayers on a voluntary basis and for a specific and defined purpose, it may not subsequently make use of that information for a different purpose, namely the reassessment of other taxpayers, in circumstances where such use will almost inevitably result in a breach of the Crown's undertaking of confidence."

2
RECORD KEEPING:
WHAT TO KEEP AND FOR HOW LONG

Legislation allows the Canada Revenue Agency (CRA) to reassess personal and corporate tax returns for up to three years following the initial date of assessment. For GST or HST returns, the CRA has up to four years. Once these deadlines have come and gone, taxpayers should not have a sense of comfort that they can purge their records. In certain cases, where there is believed to have been fraud or gross negligence on the part of the taxpayer, the CRA can examine and reassess returns outside of these time periods.

Taxpayers must keep any documents that will prove how much they earned from all sources and to substantiate their expenses. This could include receipts, credit card statements, bank statements, financial records, emails, purchase and sale agreements, legal documents, etc. Generally, records and supporting documentation needed to determine taxpayer

obligations and entitlements must be retained by the taxpayer for a period of six years. As per the *Income Tax Act* (ITA), the six-year retention period begins at the end of the tax year to which the records relate. For corporations, the tax year relates to the fiscal period, and for individual taxpayers, the tax year relates to the calendar year.

Further, there are times when records and documents must never be disposed, such as those related to the disposal of property (e.g., real estate, investments, and shares in companies) or long-term acquisitions (e.g., purchase of an apartment building for rental income or shares in a company that will be held for many years). The taxpayer must be able to prove what he or she paid for the property or acquisition so he or she can pay the correct amount of tax when it is sold. Such records and documents may include purchase and sale agreements, stock transactions, share registries, and other historical information that would have an impact on the sale or liquidation of property. Without access to such documentation at the time of a sale, the taxpayer may have to pay more than his or her fair share of taxes.

For example, if you purchase stock at $100 per share today and sell the stock at $150 per share in 20 years, you will need to prove to the CRA the price at which you initially purchased the stock so the CRA can assess capital gains based on a $50 gain per share instead of a $150 gain per share. The CRA will assume that you paid nothing for the stock (without your documentation), and that your entire sale price is profit. This is a huge departure from reality, which will cause a large difference in the tax payable, and unless you have kept all the relevant paperwork, it will be impossible to prove to the CRA that it has overassessed you.

Special circumstances trigger an additional retention period. In some situations the CRA will demand taxpayers to retain records beyond the standard retention period, either by requests made in-person by CRA officials, or by registered letter.

The following are examples of special circumstances:

- If an assessment is being objected to the CRA's Chief of Appeals, or appealed to the Tax Court of Canada following an unsuccessful objection, all records which may be necessary as proof should be kept until the six-year period has passed, or until such time as the matter has been finalized.

- If a taxpayer files a late income tax return, his or her records should be kept for six years from the date the return is assessed following filing.

- If your business or organization is unincorporated and operations have ceased to exist or operate, your records must be kept for a six-year period beginning at the end of the tax year in which operations ceased to exist or operate.

- If the taxpayer is deceased, his or her legal representative should maintain all necessary records until such time a clearance certificate is obtained from the CRA, which would then allow the distribution of property under his or her control.

- If there is a corporate merger or amalgamation, the resulting or acquiring corporation must retain business records as if the original corporations were in continuation.

- If dissolving a corporation, following the dissolution certain records must be maintained for two years, and long enough such that if the corporation is audited within the normal reassessment period (three years for income tax returns and four years for GST or HST returns), that it is able to prove its figures during an audit:

  Any record or document of the corporation that may be used to verify corporate tax entitlements or obligations.

  All other corporate documents (e.g., minute books, share registries).

CRA information circular IC78-10R5, "Books and Records Retention/Destruction,Æ is a good source for information as to what information must be retained by a taxpayer and for how long. It provides guidance to those required by law to keep books and records according to sections 230 and 230.1 of the *Income Tax Act*, section 87 of the *Employment Insurance Act*, and section 24 of the Canada Pension

Plan. For electronic records, information circular IC05-1R1, "Electronic Record Keeping," provides additional guidance for the taxpayer.

Keep in mind that there may be corporate and other provincial or federal statutes which require taxpayers to retain some documents for certain time periods. These are not addressed in these information circulars, and taxpayers should make themselves aware of the types of compliance concerns. A good place to start is by talking to a tax lawyer, tax accountant, or compliance expert.

1. The Importance of Maintaining Complete and Organized Records

There are a variety of reasons that should convince a taxpayer to maintain complete and organized records. There are laws enacted by Parliament that compel the taxpayer to keep such records in order to stay on the right side of the law. For example, I once had a client who should have kept his receipts as required to prove his expenses. About two years after his return had been processed the CRA chose to question a $1,500 receipt for a particular contractor. Since the taxpayer did not have the receipt in question, he was not able to produce it.

In most cases what would typically happen is that the auditor would deny the expense and reassess the taxpayer for additional taxes owing. In this case, however, the auditor was determined to obtain the receipt from the taxpayer — at any cost. When the taxpayer failed to provide the receipt through the auditor's use of section 231.1 of the ITA, which entitles the auditor to inspect or examine records for the purpose of administration and enforcement of the act, the auditor used his powers under sections 231.2 and 231.6 of the act, to issue a "Requirement to Provide Information." Differing from a general "Request" for information which is initially provided at the onset of the audit — and is expected to be voluntarily complied with to the best of one's ability — a "Requirement" for information under section 231.2 of the act compels a taxpayer to provide the information or possibly be charged for unlawfully failing to provide it.

As my client did not have the receipt in question, he was not able to provide it, despite the requirement. I will never know if this receipt actually existed, or whether the expense was fabricated, but my client insisted that it was a legitimate expense and that he simply did not hold onto the receipt. In the end, the auditor recommended that my client be charged as a criminal, and a summons was delivered to his home by a police officer. This is when I was approached with the grim task of defending this taxpayer in the same courtroom with drug dealers and thieves. Had my client held onto the necessary documents as required in order to satisfy the law, he would not have been left in this particular predicament.

The following requires a taxpayer to maintain complete and organized records:

- *Income Tax Act* (ITA)
- *Excise Tax Act* (ETA)
- *Excise Act*, 2001 (EA 2001)
- *Employment Insurance Act* (EIA)
- Canada Pension Plan (CPP)
- *Softwood Lumber Products Export Charge Act*, 2006 (SLPECA)
- *Air Travellers Security Charge Act* (ATSCA)

Benefits for maintaining complete and organized records include:

- Helping the taxpayer to determine what taxes are owed.

- Making it easier for a person to identify his or her sources of income.

- Acting as reminders of tax credits to be claimed and expenses to be deducted.

- In case of future audit of returns, allowing the taxpayer to substantiate and prevent disallowances of his or her expenses, and prove his or her income.

Many people are not sure of what kind of records to keep, or how they should be kept. Regardless of how much a taxpayer knows about record keeping, in order to stay on the right side of the CRA, it is best to consult the CRA document RC4409, "Keeping Records," for guidance. Everything a taxpayer could possibly want to know about record keeping is provided in this guide, and it is an invaluable resource for all businesses and self-employed individuals. It deals with paper and electronic record keeping, as well as record keeping for payroll and GST or HST.

If you keep electronic records, you may be asked to provide documents to support your entries, so it is important to also keep all of your receipts, bank statements, deposit slips, cancelled cheques, and all other important documents. Most importantly, don't find yourself in the position in which a great number of my clients have found themselves — realize that computers crash, and hard drives are temporary. Back up your business records regularly. A crashed computer without a backup can cost you thousands in extra taxes. Your lack of data gives the auditor free reign to deny all your expenses that relied on the electronic data as proof.

2. Why the CRA Is Not Fond of the Self-Employed

With the economic decline over the last few years, a great number of jobs have been eliminated, which has resulted in an increase in the number of people who are self-employed. Industry Canada's *Small Business Quarterly* shows that self-employment has increased 1.5 percent between 2008 and 2009, increasing the number of self-employed workers by 40,000 to a grand total of more than 2.6 million.

Simply put, it is easier for the CRA to keep tabs on the earnings of a taxpayer, and thus more likely for it to collect the appropriate amount of tax, if the taxpayer is not self-employed. The CRA is not fond of self-employed individuals because they are complicated and less likely to pay their fair share of taxes.

When an individual is employed, his or her employer typically makes all the necessary tax deductions at source and remits them to the CRA. Additionally, the employer provides a summary to the CRA indicating how much each employee has earned and how much tax has been withheld. As such, by the end of the year, an employee's taxes have been paid, and in many circumstances he or she is due a refund. This makes the CRA's job of administering and enforcing the ITA and collecting the taxes an easy task.

However, with self-employed individuals, the situation is never very easy or clear for the CRA. Self-employed individuals have deductions that are applied against their income, and their returns are far more complicated than simply providing and tabulating information slips provided to them by third parties. When such information slips are the sole source of a taxpayer's information to the CRA, it is very easy for the CRA to verify that the taxpayer has fully and completely disclosed his or her income. The CRA simply cross-references the information slips provided by all third parties against information provided by a taxpayer. If there is a discrepancy or a missed information slip, the CRA will know right away. In the case of a self-employed individual, the CRA would have to perform an audit in order to determine the accuracy of a return, which in turn makes the job more difficult.

If you are an employer, in order to defend yourself during an audit, and to prevent being found offside during an audit with respect to the status of your workers, it is important to determine their employment status. The employment status directly affects a taxpayer's entitlement to Employment Insurance (EI) under the *Employment Insurance Act*. It can also have an impact on how a worker is treated under other legislation such as the Canada Pension Plan (CPP), and the *Income Tax Act*. Along with income tax withheld from the employees, employers are responsible for deducting CPP contributions and EI premiums which must be remitted along with the employer's share of CPP contributions and EI premiums. Since a business does not contribute towards CPP or EI for its contractors, it is often less expensive for a company to have contractors perform work rather than employees. Further, when a business engages contractors instead of hiring employees, the employer has more flexibility in terms of terms of work (e.g., sick days, paid vacations), payment, and termination. As such, many businesses attempt to classify workers as contractors instead of employees; however, sometimes the CRA disagrees and will try to reassess the business on that basis.

An employer who fails to deduct the required CPP contributions and EI premiums may be forced to pay both the employer's share and the employee's share of any contributions and premiums owing, plus penalties and interest. So, determining the status of a worker is of the utmost importance to an employer.

In order to prevent tax fraud by claiming tax deductions which otherwise would not be available to an employee, the CRA routinely investigates cases to determine employment status.

Determination of status in Quebec is made based on the Civil Code of Quebec, while in the rest of Canada, the CRA uses a test comprised of two factors to examine the "total relationship between the worker and the payer."

In the first step, the CRA assesses the intent of the parties by examining the language from when the worker/payer relationship was first created. Slight changes in language, for instance parties agreeing to a "contract for services," signals different intent than a "contract of services." The first indicating a business relationship, while the latter is indicative of an actual employment relationship.

It is evident that clarity of intent of the type of relationship is paramount when entering into a working or business relationship. When discrepancies of intent exist, the CRA tends to favour resolution towards an employment relationship versus a business relationship. This is why, whenever possible, an agreement in writing should be created, as to help clarify any possible discrepancies of intent.

Following the first step of establishing the parties' intent, the second step verifies that parties have followed through on their intent. The CRA looks at the facts of the situation to ensure that the parties are not misusing the status of the independent contractor and in doing so it will look at all the factors discussed below.

2.1 Employee versus self-employed

It is important to understand when and in what situations one may be considered a self-employed contractor versus being labelled an employee. The circumstances of the working relationship as a whole determine the employment status. Although none of the factors are individually determinative of one's status when examining whether or not one is an employee or self-employed individual, the key question is whether or not one was engaged to perform services as a person in business on his or her own account, or as an employee. Some of the factors that help determine whether a worker is an employee or a self-employed contractor are outlined below.

2.1a Level of control the company has over the worker

The degree of control the company has over the worker is important. The more control over the worker, the more likely the worker will be seen as an employee. If the worker is a contractor, such as in the case of an independent corporate financial auditor, it is not likely that the company will be able to control that auditor like it would an employee. The company may not be able to dictate the schedule of the auditor, or how the auditor performs his or her work. Since the auditor is an independent expert, he or she will likely determine how and when to do his or her job, and which hours he or she works.

Essentially, if the payer is authorized to, and has the right or ability to control the worker, or the manner in which the work is done, or what work is to be done, then the payer will likely be considered to have control over the worker's daily tasks. Such indication of the payer exercising a high level of control may lead to a conclusion that an employment type relationship is evident.

Common indicators leading the CRA to a conclusion of an employment-type relationship include when the payer determines and controls specifics within the working relationship. Such control would be evidenced by control over what techniques and procedures the work would entail, what type of work and at what pay, whether there was any direction or training on how to complete the task, as well as control over the final work product. Essentially

the working relationship is one of a subordinate type relationship, where the worker lacks the power to necessarily effect decisions or methodologies within the relationship. Other evidence may include the worker having to ask permission of the payer to work contemporaneously with the relationship.

Self-employed contractors differ from the employer-employee relationship in that the worker maintains his or her independence and is not under the direct control and power of the payer. In fact, practically the only type of control the payer has in this situation is outlining the framework for the work, while the contractor is completely independent to work as he or she chooses. Factors which may evidence a self-employed contractor include the worker being free to complete a task in the manner he or she sees fit without any oversight by a payer. This also means that a typical contractor has no true loyalty or continuity with his or her payer, and as a result, need not ask permission to accept or reject work. It is true that a contractor is usually not obligated to refrain from working for various payers contemporaneously with his or her current payer.

2.1b Source of tools and equipment required to perform the work

If the worker also has control and ownership over his or her own equipment, he or she is more likely to be considered a self-employed contractor rather than an employee. In the example of the independent corporate auditor, it is unlikely that such a contractor would be provided with a calculator and a laptop to do his or her job. These tools would generally be provided by the contractor. Similarly, one could not imagine that a person who works on a garbage truck for an hourly wage would be required to provide his or her own garbage truck.

2.1c Ability of worker to hire assistance or subcontract the work to third parties

In the vein of a self-employed contractor having a high degree of control over his or her work, a good indication that the worker is a contractor versus an employee is his or her ability to delegate services to an assistant or a replacement. If he or she cannot hire his or her own assistance or subcontract the work to third-parties, outside a provision in the service contract which prevents such subcontracting, he or she is most likely an employee.

2.1d Degree of financial risk taken by the worker

A contractor may have to prove to the CRA in the course of an audit, that he or she operates as a business independent of the company for which it performs work. In order to do so, there may be an analysis performed of whether, like any other business, the worker was in the position where there was a financial risk, and where he or she could potentially lose money. What differentiates a contractor from an employee is that generally an employee cannot lose money. If he or she shows up to work and does his or her job, the employee gets paid. This is not so for a contractor. Many contractors have invested significant resources in tools, equipment, staff, insurance, and other business costs. This puts them in the position where there is the potential for financial risk.

3
FILING TAX RETURNS

Most people file a personal income tax return each year either because they owe taxes or because they wish to receive a refund for over-paid taxes. Those who operate corporations will also likely file a corporate tax return as well as one or more GST or HST returns per year.

The tax filing system in Canada relies on taxpayers to self-asses their income, and when filing their returns, the majority of taxpayers provide complete and accurate information. Despite the possibility of serious penalties and potential imprisonment, a great many are not so forthcoming with correct information. Some people intentionally try to avoid taxes by failing to declare all their income, or by inflating their expenses or charitable contributions, and a great many others make unintentional errors on their returns. Although the odds are against a tax-payer being audited for any given year, despite the possible upside of paying less tax by being

dishonest on one's return, the penalties can be so severe that most people don't attempt it.

While allowing the taxpayers to self-assess their income, and without having massive audit departments, the CRA is successful at collect-ing hundreds of billions of dollars per year without having more than a couple hundred convictions in court each year for failure to file returns and tax evasion.

1. The Filing Mechanics

Once the taxpayer has filed his or her return, the CRA processes it and makes a determina-tion as to whether it should be accepted as filed. CRA will then assess the return based on the return filed and on information it has obtained from employers and financial institu-tions, correcting it for obvious errors. Other times, the CRA has questions regarding certain amounts and may ask the taxpayer for clarification. Within a few weeks of filing, the CRA typically has finished processing the return and has determined a taxpayer's tax liability. At that time it issues a Notice of Assessment, which left unchallenged, dictates the amount of tax owed by a taxpayer.

A taxpayer who disagrees with CRA's assessment of a particular return may appeal the assessment. The appeals process starts when a taxpayer formally objects to the Notice of Assessment with a Notice of Objection (see Sample 1), which must be filed within 90 days of the assessment, and must explain, in writing, the reasons for the appeal along with all the related facts. The objection is then reviewed by the appeals branch of the CRA, which over the last few years has been taking in excess of nine months in order to assign an Appeals Officer — creating a very lengthy process while interest will continue to accumulate on the taxes owed.

Once the Appeals Officer has made his or her decision, the CRA may vary, confirm, or vacate the appealed assessment. If the CRA varies or confirms the assessment, the taxpayer is entitled to yet another appeal to the Tax Court of Canada, and if still unsatisfied he or she may further appeal the decision to the Federal Court of Appeal. (See Chapter 14 for more information about fighting CRA in court.)

2. Personal Income Tax Returns (T1 Return)

As noted previously in Chapter 2, a taxpayer is required to file a return if he or she owes any taxes to the CRA for the relevant reporting period, or if he or she has been requested to file by the CRA. There are also various other reasons why a taxpayer may be required to file a return:

- You owe taxes.

- CRA sends you a request to file a return.

- You and your partner (i.e., spouse or common law) are splitting pension income.

- You received Working Income Tax Benefit (WITB) advance payments.

- You disposed of capital property (e.g., you sold real estate or shares) or you had a capital gain (e.g., if a mutual fund or trust attributed amounts to you, or you are reporting a capital gains reserve you claimed on your previous year's taxes).

- You have to repay Old Age Security or Employment Insurance benefits.

- You have not repaid money withdrawn from your registered retirement savings plan (RRSP) under the Home Buyers' Plan or the Lifelong Learning Plan.

- You have to contribute to the Canada Pension Plan (CPP). This can apply if, for the previous year, the total of your net self-employment income and pensionable employment income is more than $3,500 (as of the time of this book's publication).

- You are paying Employment Insurance premiums on self-employment and other eligible earnings.

If none of the above reasons apply, you may still want to file for the following reasons:

- To claim a refund.

- To claim the Working Income Tax Benefit (WITB).

- To apply for the GST or HST credit (including any related provincial credit).

- You have incurred a non-capital loss in the previous year that you want to apply in other years.

SAMPLE 1
NOTICE OF OBJECTION

Canada Revenue Agency / **Agence du revenu du Canada**

OBJECTION – *INCOME TAX ACT*

- You can use this form to file an objection to a notice of assessment or a notice of determination issued under the *Income Tax Act*.

- Deliver or mail your completed form to the Chief of Appeals at your tax services office or tax centre.

- **Filing deadlines** – If you are an individual (other than a trust) or filing for a testamentary trust, the time limit for filing an objection is whichever of the following two dates is later: one year after the date of the return's filing deadline; or 90 days after the day we sent the notice of assessment or notice of determination. In every other case, you have to file an objection within 90 days of the day we sent the notice of assessment or notice of determination.

- **Large corporations** – In addition to providing facts and reasons for objecting, large corporations have to describe each issue and specify the relief they want for each one.

- **Collection action** – We usually postpone collection action on amounts in dispute until 90 days after we mail the Minister's decision. In some situations we will not postpone collection action on disputed amounts, such as for taxes you had to withhold and remit. In all cases, interest will continue to accrue on any amount payable.

- For more information, contact the Appeals Division at your tax services office or tax centre.

To: Chief of Appeals
Address (as shown on your notice)
....
....
....

From: Name *John Doe*
Address *123 Street*
Toronto, ON
M5V 2T2
Telephone (including area code)
Home *(416) 555-5555*   Business ( )

Name and address of any authorized representative (if applicable)
....
Telephone (including area code) ( )

Please provide the following information or enclose a copy of your notice of assessment or notice of determination.

Date of notice			Number of notice (if printed on notice)	Tax year (for T2s show fiscal period end)	Social insurance number or Business number
Year	Month	Day			

Please state the relevant facts and reasons for your objection (if you need more room, attach a separate sheet).

Your signature (or of an authorized person, if a corporation or trust is filing the objection)
J Doe

Date
Year *2 9 / 2 / 0 6* Month Day *1 1*

Privacy Act – Personal Information Bank Number CRA PPU 005

T400A (12)

Canada

- You want to or your partner (i.e., spouse or common law) wants to begin or continue to receive the Canada Child Tax Benefits payments.

- You are carrying forward or transferring the unused portion of your tuition, education, and textbook amounts.

- To report income for which you could contribute to an RRSP in order to keep your RRSP deduction limit for future years up to date.

- To carry forward the unused investment tax credit on expenditures you incurred during the current year.

- You receive the Guaranteed Income Supplement or Allowance benefits under the Old Age Security program. You can renew your benefits by filing the return by April 30. If you miss this deadline, you will have to complete a renewal form.

In Canada, personal income tax is levied on the worldwide income of individuals considered to be Canadian residents for the purposes of income tax, and also on certain types of Canadian-source income earned by non-resident individuals.

Canadian taxpayers must file their T1 Tax Return by the due date yearly. Every year the returns are due following the completion of the calendar year on April 30. If you are self-employed, or a spouse or common-law partner of a contractor, returns are due June 15. For all returns, amounts owing must be received by the CRA on or prior to April 30 to avoid being subjected to interest charges or penalties.

Individuals may determine the amounts owing by first determining their yearly taxable income. The CRA is entitled to collect the personal income tax through a variety of means, such as the following:

- Installment payments, which certain individuals are required to make every quarter throughout the year instead of paying at the end of April following the tax year.

- Deductions at source. This is where direct deductions from the pay of an individual are remitted to the CRA.

- Voluntary payments.

- Payments obtained by CRA Collections Officers.

3. Corporate Returns (T2) and Other Business Returns

While individuals file T1 income tax returns, corporations file corporate T2 returns. The type of business being operated will determine which return needs to be filed by the organization. Chapter 4 outlines the various types of business structures and their filing requirements.

4. Filing Deadlines

The following sections discuss the filing deadlines for the different types of returns. (For business income tax returns, see Chapter 4 for information about the various types of business returns and their deadlines.)

4.1 Individual income tax return

Individuals are required by subsection 150(1) of the *Income Tax Act* to file tax returns no later than April 30 for the previous year. This deadline is extended to June 15 for the previous year if the individual, or the individual's spouse or common-law partner is self-employed or carries on a business. Although the deadline is fixed, exceptions to the rule do exist:

- When the due date is not a business day, such as a holiday or weekend, returns may be submitted by the next business day.

- Non-residents filing returns under section 217 must file by June 30 for the previous year.

- Self-employed individuals, their spouses, and common-law partners must file their returns by June 15 for the previous year. This does not change the April 30 due date for any GST or HST owing.

- Deceased individuals and their surviving spouse must have their returns filed. The date is extended to six months past the death of the individual, or by the regular filing, whichever comes later.

4.2 Partnership information return

Partnership information returns that follow a fiscal period that end December 31 are filed by March 31 for the majority of partnerships. An exception to this due date is if the March 31 filing deadline falls on a public holiday or a weekend, so long as it is postmarked by the next business day, or the filing and payment are received by the CRA by the next business day, it will be considered filed on time.

4.3 T4 and T4A information returns

The deadline for employers filing T4 and T4A information returns is the end of February for the previous year. This includes filing both a T4 statement of remuneration paid, and a T4A statement of pension, retirement, annuity, and other income. Similar to other filings, should the due date fall on a public holiday or weekend, the return is due the next business day.

4.4 T5 information return

T5 statements of investment income follow similar requirements to the T4 and T4A filings. The information return must be filed no later than the last day of February for the previous tax year. The deadline may depend on where one resides and whether the due date falls on a weekend or public holiday. This is because holidays vary depending on the province or territory in which one resides, which in turn alters the predictability of the due date. The rule of thumb in such a scenario is that the information return is due the following business day.

If the business activity ends or ceases to exist, a T5 must still be filed within 30 days.

5. Consequences of Not Filing

I would say that besides avoiding being a criminal in the traditional sense by not killing somebody or not stealing a car for example, filing one's tax returns is probably the best way of avoiding obtaining a criminal record. It is so easy. File your returns and don't get a criminal record for failure to file. Unfortunately, many Canadian taxpayers simply do not get this subtle point.

Many people are scared to file because they know that they cannot afford to pay the taxes so they risk a criminal record by not filing. What they fail to realize is that not *paying* their taxes is *not* illegal; they cannot get a criminal record or be imprisoned for it. However, not *filing* their taxes *is* illegal.

The many consequences associated with unfiled or late-filed tax returns are unfortunate, and are likely to occur in most instances of late filing. In the case of unfiled returns, if taxes are payable, many CRA employees will automatically assume that the taxpayer is evading the payment of taxes by not filing his or her returns. Sometimes the CRA is right, and other times a taxpayer has every intention of paying, but gets in trouble nonetheless.

Typically, when the CRA discovers that a taxpayer has failed to a file return, it will send a letter requesting that the taxpayer file any outstanding returns. If the return is not filed by the deadline, employees at the CRA can decide to either arbitrarily assess the taxpayer (a process in which the CRA makes a guess at the tax owing — usually it is much more than the actual tax owing), in which case the taxpayer must either object or file his or her return to correct inconsistencies, or the CRA may issue a requirement to file a return. In this case, failure to produce the return can result in a referral to the Public Prosecution Service of Canada for charges, and a trip to court for a trial.

The CRA learns about failures to report income from a variety of sources including anonymous tips, information gathered from financial institutions, and other taxpayers during the course of an audit. The CRA has been known to find undisclosed earnings, such as finding information about third-parties or employees during an audit. This could include instances of bonuses being paid yet undisclosed, or other earnings that do not match between parties.

5.1 Interest accrual

If you have unreported income, you can expect to pay interest on that income. Interest accrues from the date disclosure or when the filing should have occurred. The interest rate fluctuates each quarter. It is always higher than bank interest, so using the CRA as a lender is not a wise choice. Since interest accrues from the filing due date and is compounded daily, it does not take long before your taxes become difficult or impossible to repay. Since a debt to the CRA can double in as little as seven years depending on the interest rates, you can imagine how many people have been led to financial ruin or bankruptcy as a result of late filing.

5.2 Penalty imposition

The CRA's late filing penalties are designed to be tough, and I have heard of a great deal of taxpayers who have lost their homes or who have had to declare bankruptcy because of the penalties.

If a taxpayer has not filed his or her taxes, he or she will automatically be subject to a late-filing penalty. Late-filing penalties are applied automatically when late returns are processed, although they can be reduced after the fact through a request for taxpayer relief, but they are not discretionary and outside of the protection of the Voluntary Disclosures Program (see Chapter 10 for more information).

Penalties vary depending on whether the taxpayer is a repeat offender. If penalized for the first time, the taxpayer is penalized 5 percent of the balance owing in addition to 1 percent of the balance owing for every month it is late to a maximum of 12 months. If, however, the taxpayer is a repeat offender, the penalty doubles to 10 percent of the balance owing in addition to 2 percent of the balance owing for every month it is overdue to a maximum of 20 months. Furthermore, penalties are charged interest, which are compounded daily.

5.3 Fines or imprisonment

The CRA can have the taxpayer charged for tax evasion. It can come in the form of a charge for failure to file or tax evasion. If the taxpayer is unsuccessful at trial, besides obtaining a criminal record which will follow the taxpayer for the rest of his or her life unless he or she obtains a pardon, the loss of a trial can mean serious fines of up to $25,000 per count in the case of failure to file an information return. Further, the taxpayer may be subject to being imprisoned upon a conviction, and written up on the CRA's website in the Media Room section under "Convictions."

6. Tax Preparation

Millions of tax returns are prepared each year in Canada. Many people turn to professionals to prepare their returns, and as computer literacy has increased, more people have started to prepare their own returns either online or with purchased tax software.

It does not matter how you have your return prepared or how you file — as long as the return is correct and filed on time. If you wish to manually prepare your own General Income Tax and Benefit Return, it is accessible on the CRA's website. You can download, view, and print the return. If more convenient, a hard copy of the package, as well as other CRA publications and forms, may be ordered directly from the CRA website.

6.1 Tax software

Many paid commercial and non-commercial tax preparation software packages exist in order to prepare your tax return either on your computer or online. Freeware or non-commercial tax preparation software is available online. Additionally, for the budget conscious do-it-yourselfer, tax returns may be filed online free of charge through NETFILE, a CRA run service.

In order to be sure that the software or online tool that you choose is compatible with the CRA NETFILE electronic tax filing service, you must ensure that the software chosen is CRA certified. The earliest time to check the list of certified commercial software is in late January, as the software is tested and certified by the CRA sometime between December and March. The CRA provides a list of certified software programs on their NETFILE website (netfile.gc.ca).

If you choose to use the NETFILE system or any other online filing system, keep in mind that not all returns may be filed online. You cannot file online if you —

- are in the process of bankruptcy,
- are filing for previous years (you can only file online for the current tax year),

- have never filed a tax return with the CRA before, and
- are not resident of Canada.

6.2 Using an accountant or a tax return preparer

A great many Canadians engage the services of accountants and tax return preparers each year during income tax season.

One thing to consider when you are getting help is that not all help is good help. In fact, a great deal of my clients are taxpayers who need assistance sorting matters in which their "accountant" had led them astray or given them poor advice or service. Invariably they refer to the person who was doing their taxes or handling their negotiations and dealings with the CRA as their "accountant," yet in many cases the person was not an accountant at all. Oftentimes, the client had engaged the services of somebody who was unreliable or unqualified.

"Accountant" is not a protected word, unlike the words "police officer" and "lawyer." That is to say that anybody may claim to be an accountant or may provide accounting services, even if they are not a licensed or credentialed accountant, whereas not everybody can call themselves a police officer or lawyer.

This is not to say that you should always engage a Chartered Accountant to prepare your tax returns. If your taxes are simple, you may fare much better by having a tax return preparer do your taxes. If the preparer knows what he or she is doing, the returns will likely be correct and you will pay a much lower rate than the Chartered Accountant would have charged you. However, if you have a more complicated tax return, you may want to seek the type of a tax professional that you believe would be best suited to give you advice. It may be a Certified General Accountant, a Chartered Accountant, or even a Tax Lawyer depending on the issues and the level of complexity.

As always, read your return and verify the contents before signing — regardless of who prepared it. Once you sign the return, you become liable for any inaccuracies, and you can be severely penalized or punished for false statements.

7. Things to Consider When Preparing Your Return

The following three sections discuss things you should consider when preparing your tax return or late tax returns.

7.1 Amended tax returns

Sometimes a taxpayer must file a return with all the information he or she has at the time — even though some information may come at a future date. In this case, the taxpayer is not necessarily evading taxes, but he or she is filing a return with an estimate built-in. Once the information becomes available, there is a process by which the tax return can be updated to reflect the true figures. In order to update or make changes to a personal income tax return that was previously filed, the CRA prefers that the taxpayer complete a T1 Adjustment Request (T1-ADJ) form, rather than to file an amended return. The T1-ADJ can be found on the CRA's website as well as in the offices of local tax service providers.

Once the T1 Adjustment Request is received by the CRA, it can either process it as filed, or it may choose to audit the request to verify its validity.

7.2 Waiver in respect of the normal reassessment period or extended reassessment period

Sometimes when the taxpayer requests adjustments to returns at a time when the CRA would no longer be allowed to reassess those returns because of a limitation under the law, the CRA will request that the taxpayer provide a signed waiver permitting the CRA to reassess the taxpayer outside of the allowable time. In circumstances where the taxpayer will benefit from the reassessment, he or she may consider signing the waiver, but the person should seek legal advice.

Be careful if you are going to consider signing: I have on various occasions represented clients against unscrupulous CRA auditors who had provided a waiver for my client to sign because he or she had waited too long to reassess the taxpayer, which would have made the audit a waste of time. One of those times the auditor went around my back and contacted my client directly. In cases involving an audit which had been delayed, the signing of a waiver could be detrimental to the taxpayer, except in the extreme unlikely case of the audit results being found in favour of the taxpayer. As such, a taxpayer should not sign any waiver until he or she has received proper legal advice.

7.3 If you have not filed your return

If you are not up-to-date on your filings, or you have not fully reported your income, the matter should be considered serious and attention should be focused immediately on resolving the situation. Your course of action would differ depending on whether you have been contacted by the CRA regarding your failure to file. If you have not yet been contacted by the CRA, either in writing, by telephone, or in person, it is likely that you may qualify for the Voluntary Disclosure Program, which could help you avoid penalties and prosecution (see Chapter 10 for more information).

4
BUSINESS TAXATION IN CANADA

Each year approximately 139,000 new small businesses are created in Canada. Roughly 25 percent of small businesses operate in Canadian goods-producing industries while the remaining 75 percent operate in service industries. In Canada in 2008, there were 2.6 million people who claimed self-employment income on their tax returns, which means 15 out of every 100 Canadians are self-employed. Failure rates for small businesses in Canada are high for the first three years but decline over time. About 70 percent of small businesses that enter the marketplace survive for one full year, half that total survive for three years, and approximately 25 percent are still operating after nine years.

Naturally, all businesses operating in Canada have to pay their fair share of taxes to the federal government. These taxes fall in two general categories: taxes on profit income and taxes on capital income. It is worth noting that corporate income is taxed prior to its distribution among the shareholders in the form of dividends, which in turn are taxed as personal income in the hands of the shareholders.

1. Business Structures

Under the *Income Tax Act*, a business may be taxed if it fits the working test of carrying on business for the purpose of profit. So long as that intention is supported by evidence, the business will be taxed.

A business need not be licensed or registered in any way for a person to owe taxes as a result of the business. If the person opened up a lemonade stand on a hot weekend and made $10,000, regardless of whether that business was registered or not, the CRA will want a piece of the action. Businesses may include undertakings, ventures, trade, or in short, any activity where a person is expecting a profit, and the income from that business would be taxable by the CRA.

The organizational structure chosen for the business can have a significant impact on the type of returns filed each year, the way taxes are reported, and many other taxation and business matters.

1.1 Sole proprietorship

A sole proprietorship is the default business structure for a business with one owner, unless the business owner affirmatively chooses a different business structure. As such, the sole proprietorship is a simple business structure to form and requires no legal filing to create. In a sole proprietorship, the individual and the business are one and the same for tax and legal liability purposes. Not a separate entity. Hence the term "sole" stands for single, and the term "proprietor" stands for ownership.

A sole proprietorship may be identified when the owner is the only person responsible for the decision making of the business. If the owner maintains control over decision making, profits, and losses, then in essence, the default rule is that he or she is the business. Although the person may register a business name, if the taxpayer is operating a sole proprietorship, there is no legal distinction between Andrew and "Andrew's Dog Grooming" — they are one and the same.

There are advantages to having a sole proprietorship:

- Easy to establish and maintain.

- Only one tax return must be filed; the sole proprietor is liable for the business's income on his or her personal income tax return.

- Complete control over business decisions.

- Freedom to dissolve the sole proprietorship.

The disadvantages of a sole proprietorship include:

- The sole proprietor is personally liable for the debts and obligations of the business.

- The sole proprietor is directly liable for the financial obligations of the business, including liability for claims or lawsuits.

- The sole proprietor is directly liable for taxes owed by the business. The CRA does not distinguish between collections action against the business or that of the owner.

- All of his or her personal assets are at risk.

Since there is no legal separation of the business from the one person who manages, controls, and owns it, the sole proprietor must report all income and deductible expenses for the business on his or her personal income tax and benefit return.

1.1a Tax forms for sole proprietorships

When a sole proprietorship files the income tax return, he or she must include financial statements with the return, or if applicable, the following forms:

- Statement of Business or Professional Activities (T2125) is to be completed by self-employed individuals to help report business or professional income and expenses.

- Statement of Fishing Activities (T2121) is to be completed by the self-employed fisher to help calculate fishing income and expenses.

- Statement A (T1163) is to be completed by self-employed farmers who report farming income and participate in the AgriStability and AgriInvest Programs Information and Statement of Farming Activities for Individuals.

- Statement B (T1164) is to be completed by self-employed farmers who report farming income for additional operations and participate in the AgriStability and AgriInvest Programs Information and Statement of Farming Activities for Additional Farming Operations.

- Statement A (T1273) is to be completed by self-employed farmers who report farming income and participate in the Harmonized AgriStability and AgriInvest Programs Information and Statement of Farming Activities for Individuals.

- Statement B (T1274) is to be completed by self-employed farmers who report farming income for additional operations and participate in the Harmonized AgriStability and AgriInvest Programs Information and Statement of Farming Activities for Additional Farming Operations.

- Statement of Farming Activities (T2042) is to be completed by self-employed farmers to help calculate farming income and expenses.

1.2 Partnerships

A partnership is two or more persons who carry on as co-owners of a business for a profit. When there is more than one owner and no affirmative steps have been taken to choose a different business structure, a partnership becomes the default structure. A partnership may form without the individuals being aware; for example, if you and your friend create a business and you do not incorporate it or take any steps to have a formalized business structure that is recognized by law, you will automatically by default have formed a partnership.

Similar to a sole proprietorship, a partnership is not a separate legal entity, and each partner is able to make a commitment to others (e.g., hire a subcontractor) on behalf of both partners. For example, if one partner asks a carpenter to build a table for their lemonade stand, both partners will be liable for the payment of the carpentry services even though only one of the partners hired the carpenter.

Consequently, each partner is an agent of the partnership, meaning that the action of one partner is binding on the other, which underlines the importance of having partners that you can trust. If there are any claims or judgments against the partnership, each partner is liable both jointly and severally, and may be liable to the full extent of their personal assets, to satisfy the obligations of the Canadian partnership.

Be very careful and obtain independent legal advice before entering into a partnership. It is important to know your partners and to have a very clear agreement with them as to all the terms of the partnership.

There are various forms of partnerships such as the general partnership and limited partnership, which are described in the following sections.

1.2a General partnership

In a general partnership, the business consists of two or more owners, but it is treated like a sole proprietorship for tax and legal liability purposes. Each partner is jointly and severally liable for all of the debts and obligations of the partnership. This means that each partner is personally liable for all partnership debts and obligations, even if incurred without their knowledge. Any partner may bind the partnership.

A partnership is dissolved automatically upon the death or withdrawal of a partner, if no partnership agreement exists to the contrary. Accepting a new partner, if not provided for in a partnership agreement, also calls for the automatic dissolution of the partnership. Partnership agreements may help to prevent automatic dissolution if the agreement includes a clause indicating that a vanishing partner's interest may be purchased by the surviving partner.

1.2b Limited partnership

In a limited partnership, the business consists of two or more owners, at least one of which must be a general partner, and at least one must be a limited partner. The limited partnership is treated like a sole proprietorship for tax purposes, but like a corporation for liability purposes.

The general partner is treated as if he or she is in a general partnership, has unlimited liability, and is personally liable for the debts and obligations of the partnership. The limited partner, however, has limited liability so long as he or she does not control any aspect of the partnership.

Unlike a general partnership, a limited partnership does not occur automatically and must be formed according to statute. For instance, according to the Ontario *Limited Partnerships Act*, a limited partnership must be formed by filing a declaration with the registrar.

1.2c Tax and filing requirements for partnerships

The following outlines the taxation and filing requirements for a partnership:

- The partnership itself is not its own entity and does not pay income tax.

- Individual partners pay tax earned from the partnership on their individual T1

income tax returns by completing Statement of Business or Professional Activities (T2125).

- As a corporate partner, the taxpayer will report business income in his or her T2 corporate income tax return.

- If during a fiscal year the partnership has at least six partners, further filing requirements must be met. Beyond individual partners completing Statement of Business or Professional Activities (T2125) so too must the partnership complete a Partnership Information Return (PIR) and Statement of Partnership Income (T5013).

- If relevant, each partner may also be required to file the following forms or file financial statements:

  - Statement of Fishing Activities (T2121) is to be completed by self-employed fisher to help calculate fishing income and expenses.

  - Statement of Business or Professional Activities (T2125) is to be completed by self-employed individuals to help report business or professional income and expenses.

  - Statement A (T1163) is to be completed by self-employed farmers who report farming income and participate in the AgriStability and AgriInvest Programs Information and Statement of Farming Activities for Individuals.

  - Statement B (T1164) is to be completed by self-employed farmers who report farming income for additional operations and participate in the AgriStability and AgriInvest Programs Information and Statement of Farming Activities for Additional Farming Operations.

- Statement A (T1273) is to be completed by self-employed farmers who report farming income and participate in the Harmonized AgriStability and AgriInvest Programs Information and Statement of Farming Activities for Individuals.

- Statement B (T1274) is to be completed by self-employed farmers who report farming income for additional operations and participate in the Harmonized AgriStability and AgriInvest Programs Information and Statement of Farming Activities for Additional Farming Operations.

- Statement of Farming Activities (T2042) is to be completed by self-employed farmers to help calculate farming income and expenses.

1.3 Corporations

The corporation is a very popular and important vehicle for conducting business in Canada as it comes with a number of major advantages, arguably the most important of which is the fact that a corporation has its own identity under the law, separate from its owners or directors. As such, a corporation can shield owners and directors from liabilities. A large judgment and bankruptcy of the corporation does not necessarily mean a bankruptcy of the owners or directors. While certain corporate debts can be assigned to the directors of the corporation, such as unpaid GST or HST and payroll remittances, in general, the directors are personally shielded from virtually every other corporate debt and obligation.

In Canada, a corporation is a separate and distinct legal entity from its owners/shareholders, officers, and employees. The owners are shielded from personal liability for the debts of the corporation, but the corporation as its own legal entity must pay taxes. Only after-taxed income may be paid as dividends to shareholders. Dividends are then subject to double taxation, being taxed again as personal income to the shareholders.

Canadian corporations can gain advantages from a tax perspective in several ways. Canadian corporations are eligible for various types of tax credits and business deductions. Furthermore, a corporation in Canada can reduce taxes payable by paying income to the owners as salary rather than dividends. The corporation can deduct the salaries from its income when determining its income subject to tax. So a corporation could theoretically pay all its income back in the form of expenses and salaries and owe no taxes at the end of the year.

There is also a tax deferral created by leaving funds in the corporation. Since a corporation pays a lower tax rate than an individual, by earning income and leaving it inside the corporation, rather than withdrawing the income immediately and paying personal taxes in addition to the corporate tax, the shareholders can defer paying their personal taxes to a later date when they actually pay themselves from the corporation. This deferral of tax saves the taxpayer money because it allows the money to earn interest or be invested by the corporation until it is paid to the shareholder. Rather than being given over to the CRA right away, the tax dollars can be used to the benefit of the corporation and its owners.

There are different categories of corporations in Canada, and it is the type of corporation which ultimately determines the corporation's tax rates and treatment under the law.

Canadian controlled private corporation (CCPC):

- Is a private corporation.

- Is not controlled by public corporations, even if indirectly, unless considered to be a venture capital corporation per Regulation 6700.

- Is controlled by Canadian residents or is incorporated in Canada since June 18, 1971, to the end of the tax year.

- Is not controlled by a non-resident, even if indirectly.

- Is not controlled by a resident corporation which publicly trades stock outside of Canada.

- Capital stock is not traded publicly on stock exchanges.

Other private corporation:

- Is a private corporation.

- Is a resident in Canada.

- Is not controlled by federal Crown corporations, per Regulation 7100.

- Is not controlled by public corporations, unless considered to be a venture capital corporation per Regulation 6700.

Public corporation:

- Has one or more classes of shares on a designated stock exchange in Canada or per Regulation 4800(1) is designated as a public corporation.

- Financial exposure of the shareholder is limited to the share purchase price, risking no more than the amount paid for the stock, or the value of the asset transferred to the corporation in exchange of the shares.

2. Goods and Services Tax (GST) and Harmonized Sales Tax (HST)

While income taxes are governed by the *Income Tax Act*, The Goods and Services Tax (GST) and the Harmonized Sales Tax (HST) are governed by the *Excise Tax Act*. GST and HST are taxes that apply on the supply of most goods and services made in Canada. In provinces where the HST is not in force, a 5 percent GST is applied to the price of goods and services.

In provinces where the HST is in force, the 5 percent GST has been added to a provincial tax amount, providing for varying HST rates from province to province. Five provinces have harmonized their provincial sales tax with GST to create HST. At the time of writing, Nova Scotia has the highest HST rate of 15 percent; followed by Ontario, New Brunswick, and Newfoundland and Labrador, which are 13 percent; and British Columbia at 12 percent. (**Note:** BC will discontinue using HST and return to the separate PST and GST system as of April 1, 2013.) These rates are affected by both the federal (GST) portion and the provincial portion, and are subject to change.

Upon selling goods and services which are subject to the GST or HST (some products and services such as milk, bread, prescription drugs, and certain transportation services are not subject to GST or HST), the vendor of the goods or services must charge the appropriate tax rate, which is ultimately based on the province in which the purchaser is located.

With the exception of Status Indians and provincial and territorial governments other than BC and Ontario (which have agreed to pay GST or HST on their purchases), consumers of taxable supplies of goods and services, regardless of whether the purchaser is a business or a person, are required to pay GST or HST. If a business is a GST or HST registrant, it can claim back all the GST or HST that it has paid. Diplomats and consulates are required to pay the GST or HST at the time of purchase, but they are able to receive a GST or HST rebate.

Suppliers of goods and services, whom are also GST or HST registrants, must collect GST or HST on all taxable goods and services they provide to their customers. Exceptions exist for zero-rated supplies and also for the taxable sale of real property. A supply that is zero-rated has a 0 percent GST or HST rate. Such supplies include basic groceries, agricultural products such as grain, prescription drugs, and medical devices such as hearing aids. Generally, if one imports or supplies in goods and services in Canada, those supplies are subject to GST or HST at varying rates or are zero-rated.

The following are some examples of goods and services that are subject to GST or HST:

- Auto mechanic services
- Fuel or gasoline
- Vehicle rentals or sales
- Spa services
- Legal services
- Snack foods and candy
- Hotel or room rental
- Commercial real property rental or sale

The following are some examples of goods and services that are zero-rated:

- Supplies or services solely provided for the Governor General
- Prescription drugs and related dispensing fees

- Staple grocery items
- Most fishery products and farm livestock made for human consumption
- Exports and various international transportation services
- Exempt goods and services

Exempt goods and services are related to specified GST or HST exempt goods. The supplier of such goods does not charge GST or HST to the supplier's customers. Furthermore, exempt goods and services are not claimed, so there is no need to file an input tax credit (ITC).

The following are examples of exempt goods and services:

- Services for legal aid
- Some educational services and child-care services
- Condominium fees if for residential use and residential housing if long term
- Many goods and services provided by charities and non-profit organizations
- Many health- or medical-related services provided by licensed medical doctors

3. Payroll Taxes

Employers are responsible for deducting Canada Pension Plan (CPP) contributions, Employment Insurance (EI) premiums, and personal income tax from the remuneration of the employees. The employers must remit these amounts to the CRA and report them on the applicable slips as well.

When a business runs into trouble with the CRA, along with GST and HST, it is generally payroll taxes that cause problems. Unlike corporate taxes, which must be paid at the end of the year if a business is profitable, GST or

HST and payroll tax monies are referred to as "trust" monies and must be remitted whether or not a business is profitable. That is to say, that the business collects these monies on an ongoing basis on behalf of the government, and holds them in trust to be remitted on a certain schedule. The CRA expects that these monies are held aside in a separate account, and are never touched by the business. The problem is that when businesses start to run into financial difficulties, one of the first things business owners do is dip into the GST or HST monies that the business has received from clients, and using the funds to meet the business expenses.

Additionally, as a cost-saving measure, the business will stop remitting payroll taxes in order to keep its expenses down. In the case of payroll taxes, the amounts paid to the employees in their paycheques do not reflect the true cost of the employees. For example, if an employee lives in Ontario and earns $32,000 per year, his or her federal income taxes for 2012 would be 15 percent or $4,800, and his or her provincial income taxes would be 5.05 percent or $1,616. To keep the employee working, the employer must pay the employee $25,584 (less the employee's EI and CPP contributions), but the employer is also required to pay the CRA $6,416. When a business struggles, the owner chooses not to terminate the employees, but instead "borrow" from the CRA to finance the business by failing to remit the payroll taxes. As you can imagine, it is far easier to come up with $25,584 to pay the employee rather than the full $32,000, and by not remitting the payroll taxes, the employer can keep his or her employee working and temporarily save $6,416. Most business owners who start to finance their business on CRA remittances are delusional and believe that they will be able to catch up and pay the monies back when business improves. However, these savings do not last for long.

Once the remittances stop or start to lag behind schedule, the CRA becomes very aggressive with the collections of both payroll taxes and GST or HST, and regardless of whether the business is going to improve, often the business is not given the time to improve because of the harsh collections action which ensues. Corporate bank accounts become frozen, assets are seized, and the CRA will collect monies owed to the company directly from its clients by issuing a "requirement to pay." Within weeks, such collection actions deprives the business of any funds which in turn prevents it from paying its employees and suppliers, and which can very quickly lead to the premature bankruptcy of the corporation. When a corporation fails, the CRA begins to pursue directors of the corporation personally for the unpaid trust debts, causing many of them to have to lose their homes and even declare personal bankruptcy.

As such, one of the best pieces of advice I can give any employer is the following: When a business starts to fail, never ever use trust monies to keep it going. *Never.* Instead, in order to avoid a catastrophic failure, a business must either borrow money from a financial institution or reduce its cost structure and possibly layoff staff.

Employers must follow certain requirements when they pay wages or salaries, such as register a payroll account. A payroll account is also needed should the employer provide benefits, allowances, gratuities, or even vacation pay. If the employer is reporting, remitting, and deducting, then the employer requires a payroll account. A payroll account may be created and added to the business number (BN). If the employer doesn't have a BN, he or she must ensure that a request for a payroll account and registration has occurred prior to the due date of the first remittance.

Employers have certain responsibilities to perform:

- Reporting on the T4 information return employees' remuneration and deductions and providing information slips to the employees.

- Remitting deductions including the amounts paid on the employees' behalf of EI premiums and CPP or QPP contributions.

- Deducting from the amounts paid to the employees' income tax, EI premiums, and CPP or QPP contributions.

4. Canada Pension Plan (CPP) and Quebec Pension Plan (QPP)

Every worker in Canada is entitled to financial assistance through Canada Pension Plan (CPP) benefits when they retire. Similarly, businesses operating in Quebec must make payroll deductions for Quebec Pension Plan (QPP) contributions rather than CPP, remitting payments not to the Receiver General, but instead to Revenu Quebec. CPP or QPP contributions must be deducted by employers from the pensionable earnings of the employees. Employees must then contribute the additional employer's portion — so both employees and employers make contributions to the CPP or QPP systems.

5. Employment Insurance (EI)

When people become unemployed, generally through no fault of their own, they may be eligible to receive temporary federal assistance by applying for Employment Insurance (EI). It is the duty of every employer to ensure EI premiums are deducted from employees' insurable earnings, of which the rates for EI premiums may vary from year to year.

In addition to the contributions made by employees, employers must on the employees' behalf make their own EI contributions, which are usually larger than the employees' contributions. Employers are responsible for remitting CPP premiums and income taxes deducted, as well as remitting EI premiums to the CRA on a regular basis.

Remittances by employers are generally required monthly. The larger the business, the more likely remittances must be made more frequently. For instance, a small employer may be permitted to make only quarterly remittances, while large employers will be required to remit tax and payroll deductions on a more frequent basis.

6. Trusts

A trust is either a testamentary trust or an inter vivos trust — different tax rules apply to each type.

6.1 Testamentary trust

A testamentary trust is a trust created by a will. It is considered a personal trust and does not commence during the lifetime of the individual (i.e., the settlor) whom set up the trust; the trust or trust estate is only created upon death of the settlor. Testamentary trusts usually only come into existence by the deceased individual, and may not include a trust created later than November 12, 1981, if property was transferred to the trust other than by the settlor upon his or her death. The deceased's will governs the testamentary trust terms so long as it is within the bounds of applicable provincial statute, and sometimes a court order is needed to help ensure the estate property is adequately prescribed.

The testamentary trusts first taxation period begins the day following the settlor's death.

This taxation period must end sometime before the end of the 12th month; the exact date being at the discretion of the trustee. Trustees may choose to elect a fiscal period, such as the calendar year, to help simplify accounting. Others may wish to maximize tax deferral by making use of the full 12-month taxation period following the settlor's death. Should a trustee wish to change the taxation period of a testamentary trust, he or she must do so with the permission of the Minister of National Revenue.

6.2 Inter vivos trust

The inter vivos trust is used for estate planning purposes and is created during the lifetime of the trustor. Also known as a living trust, an inter vivos trust is in operation for a period of time as determined by the trustor during the creation of the trust. Such trusts can provide for distribution of assets to beneficiaries both during and after the lifetime of the trustor, and are often established to avoid the process of probate, which often becomes an expensive process and which may expose private financial details to public eyes as certain court documents become a matter of public record. Further, a properly established inter vivos trust can provide for assets to be distributed to intended recipients in a timely fashion without having to wait for the courts.

Both trusts and their beneficiaries may be subject to tax under sections 104 to 108 of the *Income Tax Act*. For tax purposes, under subsection 104(2) of the act, trust estates are considered to be their own entity. Depending on the purpose of the trust, it may carry on business, own property, and earn taxable income. Similar to other taxpaying entities, it too is subject to income tax. Taxation is separated between income taxable at death of the deceased, which the deceased estate is responsible for, and income earned later by the trust property. There is an exception under subsection 164(6) of the act, which allows the estate to transfer capital losses and terminal losses incurred during its first taxation year against the deceased's income in the year of death.

In order to prevent double-taxation of the trust and the beneficiaries who are in receipt of trust funds, the trust estate may at times flow the income through the trust directly to its beneficiaries, claiming deductions for those amounts. This may occur either when income becomes payable to the trust beneficiaries, or when actual income is distributed to the trust beneficiaries.

The tax year for inter vivos trusts has a firm requirement and must coincide with the calendar year (see subsections 104(2) and 249(1) of the *Income Tax Act*), whereas, a testamentary trust need not coincide with the calendar year. For the testamentary trust, according to subsection 104(23) of the act, the taxation year may follow any period used by the trustee or which is customary by practice, but not to exceed 12 months.

5
TAX AUDITS AND REVIEWS

There are few words that scare a taxpayer more than "you have been selected for an audit." For some, it is because they have either understated their income or overstated their expenses, and it is more than likely that people in this category will be caught by an audit. A few of these individuals will be charged criminally with tax evasion and some may face imprisonment. Still more will be assessed with extra tax that should have already been paid, gross negligence penalties of 50 percent of the tax owing, and daily interest on both amounts.

The reason that most people are fearful of being audited is because, although they have filed their income tax returns honestly and to the best of their (or their tax return preparer's) ability, they know that they have to completely open themselves to the prying and watchful eyes of the auditor and sit back while every detail of their lives is scrutinized. From the

amount a taxpayer spends on food, to whom is responsible for taking care of his or her children, to personally examining the taxpayer's home office — everything is subject to being examined by an auditor. The taxpayer has very little choice but to cooperate — usually causing great anxiety — even on the part of the most honest taxpayer. Although most people complete their returns honestly to a great extent, many of them know that there is some sort of a defect in their paperwork or record keeping that will be uncovered by the Canada Revenue Agency (CRA) that may cause them to be reassessed and owe extra taxes.

Whether a taxpayer has been audited previously or not, he or she has heard of audits and their outcomes. People know that audits result in extra taxes owing. Whether it is a missing or misplaced receipt, a package of documents that were never returned by an accountant, misplaced documents during a move, lost in the mail, or even lost because of a crashed hard drive, most people do have some sort of a problem substantiating all their expenses during an audit, or have a defect in their returns, which invariably is uncovered through an audit.

The problem is that most Canadians do not know how to approach an audit. Many still think that an audit is simply an opportunity for the CRA to verify the data on the taxpayer's return. After all, it is a self-reporting system, and in order to keep us honest, the CRA needs to randomly check in on a bunch of us to make sure we got it right! A great many people still believe that if they have been honest on their return, the auditor will not assess them for any extra taxes. The auditor is not the enemy, people believe, they have no vested interest in making them pay more taxes than they should. This could not be further from the truth.

Simply put, the job of the auditors is to make money for the CRA. Auditors have to justify their existence or the CRA would not spend millions of dollars per year employing them. Those auditors who audit individuals and small- and medium-sized businesses all earn money for the CRA — each and every one of them, each and every year. In fact, auditors pay their salaries many times over in extra taxes, penalties, and interest recovered as a result of their audits.

According to the CRA's "Annual Report to Parliament" (for 2006 to 2007), on average, each personal audit resulted in an average of $6,800 in taxes, and each GST audit resulted in an additional $9,500. What has to be understood by Canadian taxpayers is that these auditors are judged based on the amount of extra taxes they have found per hour they have worked. They are not working for fun, and the CRA reports their progress to Parliament each year.

If you put yourself in the mindset of the CRA employees, they do not earn a financial commission for extra taxes they assess, yet they want to earn raises and advance in their careers. The best way to achieve those goals is to make a name for themselves within the agency by finding as many tax dollars as they can, and by beating out their peers for the promotions. Auditors do this by being tough and meticulous — by uncovering every defect in a return, every missing receipt, and every unaccounted dollar deposited into a taxpayer's account.

This brings me to my next piece of very important advice which applies to every Canadian taxpayer, and which could potentially save you thousands of dollars during an audit: If you ever deposit any amount into your bank account, which is not income, you must make a note of it in a journal, keep a copy of the cheque deposited, and attach a copy of any supporting documentation showing why you received the cheque. For example, you may have received a cheque from an insurance company as a result of a claim for damage sustained by your vehicle during an accident, or you may have been issued a reimbursement for prescription drugs or a dental visit, or perhaps you were given a large gift from a family member, or maybe your business paid you a large amount for materials you purchased for a job. In each of these cases, the amounts received should not have been taxable. However, if these amounts are uncovered by an auditor upon inspection of the deposits to your account, and if you cannot prove that these amounts are not your earnings, the auditor will assume that they are your earnings, and you will be assessed taxes on those amounts — without proper paperwork, it will be difficult to convince the auditor otherwise.

1. Risk Factors That Increase the Odds of Being Audited

People always ask me what the chances are of them being audited, and I always answer that it depends on who you are and the risk factors.

There are two ways a taxpayer can be selected for an audit: Either randomly or through a targeted selection process. The selection process relies on the risk factors, and the random one relies on luck. The CRA's targeting process appears to be successful at finding those who are more likely to owe additional taxes based on the fact that 10 percent of taxpayers randomly selected faced an additional tax bill of more than $5,000, and 35 percent of taxpayers specifically targeted for audit faced an additional tax bill of more than $5,000.

It doesn't matter whether you have filed your Canadian tax return online or on paper, some tax audits are impossible to avoid. Each year the CRA routinely reviews random returns from various industries, and most audits are to verify that the returns were prepared correctly and honestly. Besides the random audits, which taxpayers cannot avoid, other audits are caused by errors made by the taxpayers on their returns. The more errors a taxpayer has, the greater the odds of being audited.

Besides making an error on a return, there are various different risk factors for an audit, and each taxpayer has a different set of these risk factors. If the taxpayer works as an employee for an employer, whether or not he or she contributes to RRSPs, the likelihood of an audit is very low because he or she does not have many of the risk factors. The more deductions the taxpayer has for medical expenses, tuition, child-care, etc., the greater his or her chance of being audited, but even with some of these expenses and deductions, employees receiving T4 slips each year are low risk, and thus not audited frequently. Further, since taxes are already deducted at source and remitted to the CRA, and since the CRA has been informed about income and deduction amounts by the employer, the CRA has already verified the employment income, and all the interest the person has received from investments. The CRA knows that there is likely no additional tax which can be earned by auditing the taxpayer. In short, there is nothing much for the CRA to gain by auditing an employee unless the person earns tips or commissions or has a side business.

People who are self-employed are in the high-risk category, and at especially high risk are those taxpayers who either have cash-oriented businesses, or those who fall into certain industries such as construction, which is historically notorious for cash payments and tax evasion.

What automatically puts self-employed individuals into the high-risk category is a combination of factors. Firstly, and probably most concerning to the CRA, is that these taxpayers have no employer which has already provided details of their income to the CRA and which has already paid their income tax for the year. For these taxpayers, the CRA is in the position where it has to both verify the amounts on the returns by choosing certain taxpayers for audit, and collect the taxes owed. Additionally, the fact that self-employed individuals pay taxes on the difference between their income and their business expenses, they have a vested interest to show their expenses as being as high as they can, while making their income appear as low as they can. This means that the CRA has a vested interest in verifying the numbers. The CRA has to classify every dollar deposited to the taxpayer's account as income, and denying for any variety of reasons as many taxpayer expenses as can be done within the boundaries of the CRA guidelines.

The following are some interesting facts from the CRA's "Annual Report to Parliament" (2006 to 2007):

- The CRA conducted 366,260 audits of small- and medium-sized businesses. Those audited resulted in more than $2.5 billion in additional taxes, interest, and penalties being assessed.

- The CRA conducted approximately 63,000 GST and HST audits, which resulted in tax assessments totalling more than $600 million.

- More than 1,000 CRA employees worked full-time on identification, audit, or enforcement activities to address the underground economy. They conducted 20,635 underground economy audits resulting in assessments totalling more than $284 million of additional tax.

- 98 per cent of tax evasion charges prosecuted by the CRA resulted in convictions. The CRA's conviction rate has never fallen to less than 94 percent in the past five years.

The CRA uses an automated system to help evaluate self-employed taxpayers and GST registrants. The Compliance Measurement Profiling and Assessment System (COMPASS) takes into account hundreds of factors that qualify as being high risk.

In no particular order, below are a number of risk factors which will increase a taxpayer's odds of being audited. (See sections **1.1** to **1.20** for additional targeted areas.)

- Professional income
- Audit of one's spouse
- Audit of one's business
- Audit of one's business partner or associate

- Farming income
- Fishing income
- Partnership income
- Investment income
- Purchase and sale of real estate
- Dividends from private corporations
- Support payments and alimony
- Moving expenses
- Clergy residence deduction
- Adoption expenses
- Medical expenses
- Disability support payments
- Disability tax credits
- Research and development expenses
- Investment tax credits

Other than filing a Determination of Residency Status (NR73), breaking all residential ties and leaving the country, there are a few ways to reduce the chances of being audited by the CRA. One way is to stop being self-employed and take a job, and another is to understand what the CRA is looking for and what might trigger an audit, which are addressed in the following sections.

1.1 Excessive expenses and deductions

Any time there is the possibility to uncover overstated expenses and deductions, there is the potential for a targeted audit, but in particular if you are self-employed and your overall expenses appear to be too large (upwards of 50 percent of your income), you could reasonably expect to be audited. That is unless you are in an industry where similar taxpayers have similarly large expenses relative to their income.

1.2 Major changes in income or expenses from year-to-year

The CRA does not like unpredictable taxpayers because they are more difficult to deal with. Further, unpredictable taxpayers are suspicious. When taxpayers have been consistently filing certain levels of revenues, or certain levels of expenses, with consistent expense-to-revenue ratios, and then suddenly they make a filing which indicates a sudden, dramatic change in their income or expenses, they can expect that they may be red-flagged by the computer for an audit.

1.3 A business that has repeated losses

Particular scrutiny is drawn to businesses which appear to be going nowhere. No one aims to have several years of consecutive losses, but once a person has hit three in a row, he or she should anticipate an assessment. Like the creditors, the CRA expects to see a company producing more income each year, while reducing the losses at the same time.

The reason behind this is that business losses can be used to reduce the taxpayer's taxes owing for other income so many people choose to operate money-losing businesses which provide them with certain benefits including a loss which they can use to decrease their income tax payable. The CRA wants to collect as much tax as possible, and money-losing businesses reduce tax payable.

The CRA's policy during an audit is to deny expenses for businesses which are losing money if the CRA deems that the business has no chance of making a profit. The CRA does this by declaring that a business does not exist and thus business expenses do not apply. This can happen even if the business is actually generating revenue, but just not enough to meet its expenses. The CRA defines a business as "an activity that you conduct for profit or with a reasonable expectation of profit." So, if a CRA auditor in his or her expert business opinion (remember, he or she is a government employee and has never likely started a business of his or her own) deems that your business idea is crazy, or that you will never generate a profit, he or she can apply his or her discretion to deny all of your business expenses — which in turn makes the business less profitable and more likely to fail. After all, if a business cannot claim its expenses, it will be unfairly taxed, and may likely fail on that basis alone.

If the CRA were to apply the same policy it uses to deny expenses of small, start-up businesses to the auto manufacturers of the last few years, it would have appeared that they too did not have a reasonable expectation of a profit, and thus were not running a business, and in turn, the expenses claimed could not possibly have been legitimate "business expenses" and should have been denied. However, the CRA's logic breaks down when this comparison is drawn, and its credibility breaks down even further when somebody like a young, inexperienced auditor, or an older jaded auditor is allowed to briefly examine a business and determine single-handedly, based on what little he or she has seen, that the business has no reasonable expectation of a profit and thus deny all its expenses.

1.4 Expenses that are not similar to others in your industry

The CRA routinely makes comparisons between returns of taxpayers in the same industry. If it determines that a taxpayer's expenses are grossly different from what would be expected of a taxpayer in that particular industry, this could be a cause for an audit. For example, if most restaurants have a cost of food of about 30 percent of sales, a restaurant which claims to have a food cost of 60 percent of sales may be red-flagged for an audit. Or, if a taxpayer runs a nightclub, and that nightclub has revenues that are 50 percent less than all other nightclubs of a similar size in the same area, this night club may be red-flagged for an audit.

1.5 Underreported earnings

The CRA knows about some unreported earnings because of treaties, anonymous tips, and audits of third parties which uncover payments to taxpayers who never declared them. Sometimes the CRA just has a suspicion about unreported earnings for some reason or another.

Cash industries are inherently suspicious. Cash is untraceable if handled properly. Many business owners take a certain percentage of the cash earned by their business and don't deposit it into their accounts, and never declare it. The CRA knows just how easy it is for taxpayers to conveniently fail to declare such earnings, and each year as a result, businesses in a variety of industries (e.g., construction, taxi, food-service and child-care) are subject to heightened scrutiny.

The CRA routinely embarks on special projects where it has determined there is the potential for abuse of the tax system and more importantly, where there is a strong likelihood of uncovering hidden tax dollars. For instance, high on the watch list are trades related to Alberta's thriving real estate economy (i.e., agents' expenses and the construction industry). Other hot spots that have become the subject of certain recent CRA review projects include condo pre-sales and property flipping in Vancouver and Toronto.

The CRA's focus is constantly shifting, and if you become part of a group of taxpayers who are engaged in a certain business activity, have participated in certain types of transactions, or made certain types of investments that have been determined by the CRA to have a strong likelihood of having unreported income, the odds are much higher that you will be audited as part of the CRA's program.

1.6 Lifestyle analysis

One of the sneakiest ways the CRA can detect unreported income is by examining a taxpayer's lifestyle without the person suspecting. Auditors have been known to come by and look at the types of cars in the driveway and what kind of jewellery the taxpayer is wearing. While walking through a taxpayer's home to inspect his or her home office, auditors have been known to look around for expensive electronics, fine furnishings, and any other indications of a lavish lifestyle. Their goal is to determine by the clothes the person wears or the car the person drives, whether their reported income is enough to sustain the taxpayer's lifestyle. Although CRA auditors are still trained to look around for visual signs of tax evasion during a visit, as technology and government databases with taxpayer information are becoming more advanced, they are facilitating increasingly sophisticated assessment techniques to predict who cannot afford their lifestyle and who may have unreported income.

For instance, it is possible for the CRA to check postal codes to identify individuals who appear to be living beyond their means in neighbourhoods they likely cannot afford. Many records, such as bank and credit records, or even automobile registrations can also be easily cross-referenced electronically to determine those who appear to be living beyond their means or have bank accounts larger than they should have, and who are thus likely to be failing to declare part of their income.

1.7 Large charitable donations

Large charitable donations are suspicious, particularly when they represent a large portion of a taxpayer's income. I have provided many consultations for people who have had problems with charitable donations. In many cases I have spoken to people who were audited for making donations that would appear to be 30 to 40 percent of their income. For somebody earning a million dollars per year, they could likely afford this, but for somebody who earns $32,000 per year, it is unreasonable to accept that they have actually made a donation to charity in the amount of $13,000. After the individual has his or her taxes deducted at source, he or she only takes home about $25,000 or so, and to give $13,000 of that to a charity would mean that the individual would have had to live on $12,000 in that year — a very unlikely possibility. The more likely possibility is that either the charitable receipt is forged, or there is no receipt at all, or the taxpayer has participated in some sort of a charitable scam where he or she has donated a certain amount of money, which by some means had resulted in an inflated receipt for far greater than the actual cash paid. Either way, the CRA is right to be suspicious, and if a taxpayer plans on making a claim on the return for a charitable contribution that would appear to be large enough to cause suspicion by the CRA, it would be wise to very carefully consider which charity he or she is donating to in order to ensure that everything is legitimate, and to keep all relevant receipts and cancelled cheques. Failure to do so could be very costly.

1.8 Tax shelters and gifting programs

The CRA audits all gifting programs, and in recent years they have taken action to shut down a number of organizations who were running the programs. In the process, a number of charitable registrations were also revoked and taxpayer participants had many millions of dollars of penalties applied to their accounts.

The CRA is particularly interested in tax shelters and gifting programs, so taxpayers are advised to stay clear of them. Any type of aggressive tax planning is subject to being audited by the CRA, and one particularly tough problem arises when taxpayers participate in a tax shelter or a donation scheme which involves a charity which has a valid registration number at the time of the donation, but which later loses its registration due to infractions of tax law. Once these registration numbers are lost, the CRA will typically audit taxpayers who had donated to the affected charity over the last few years.

There have been so many different types of gifting arrangements over the years, from comic books, to medication, to posters and artwork, to education materials and software. What they all have in common is that they do not work and are not supported by Canadian law. In each of these types of schemes, participants purchase items is some way or another, and these items, which are worth far more than the purchase price are donated to a charity for a receipt indicating the market value of the items — not the amount that the taxpayer paid. There are new schemes cropping up all the time, each claiming to be legitimate and unlike its predecessors — and each one will fail. As a general rule, if a receipt shows a value that is higher than the actual cash outlay, one can expect to be audited and to lose. Recent court decisions have allowed the CRA to give the taxpayer credit for the actual cash paid out and no more. So if a large refund has been received by a taxpayer because of participation in such a scheme, he or she can expect to have to repay the amount, with penalties and interest.

Canada's tax laws are designed to allow taxpayers to contribute before-tax dollars to charity. This means that they get a credit for their donation, and their donation dollars go further. In short, they are able to donate more to charity than they would were they required to pay tax on their money before donating to charity. The laws are meant to facilitate donations, not to provide a benefit from making a donation. So if the taxpayers are offered a benefit for making a donation — other than feeling good about themselves — they should expect unequivocally, that their participation will eventually result in their being audited. If a tax shelter or a donation scheme appears too good to be true, it probably is.

1.9 Child-care costs

It is highly recommended prior to claiming child-care expenses that parents verify their documentation, and if they cannot obtain proper documentation to support the claim for expenses, they should consider not making the claim at all. The CRA is skeptical of parents abusing the system by attempting to include or write off ineligible costs, such as cash-only deals, or attempting to write off, as a babysitter cost, a relative who has not yet reached the qualifying age of 18.

1.10 Home office deductions

It seems that virtually everybody has a home office these days. Some work entirely from home, some have a small business on the side from home, and others have a place of business and still use part of their home as an office. The CRA is well aware of this growing movement, which is why they are not taking lightly those attempting to abuse the system. The CRA is known to look very carefully at claims for home office expenses, looking specifically for those write-offs that are too large, such as

too great a portion of heat, electricity, maintenance, home mortgage interest, property tax, and other carrying costs.

When working from home, it is important to note that only the business-related portions of your expenses may be deducted. Generally, such deductions are limited to 15 to 20 percent of the overall square footage of your home. On occasion, when you live in a particularly small space, your home office may occupy more than 20 percent of the floor space. In general, claims for more than 15 to 20 percent are a strong indicator that your return may be flagged for audit.

Of particular interest to the CRA is when the taxpayer fails to include the required Statement of Employment Expenses (T777) to allow for deductions of home office expenses.

1.11 Evidence of Criminal Activity

The CRA really does not care what a person does for a living. All it cares about is receiving a percentage of the profits. So whether somebody is a drug dealer or a dentist, to the CRA it does not matter. (See the CRA fact sheet "Proceeds of Crime are Taxable" for further information on taxation of proceeds of crime or illegal activity.)

What does matter is that the CRA knows that most criminals do not declare their profits. There is an enormous amount of tax loss for these criminal businesses. When the CRA catches wind of the existence of criminal activity, its goal is to learn more about it and tax it. The CRA receives information from different sources concerning criminal activity, including law enforcement agencies and stories from the news.

Designed to "conduct audits and undertake other civil enforcement actions on individuals known or suspected of deriving income from illegal activities," the Special Enforcement Program is a tool that the CRA has to obtain tax dollars from illegal activities. According to the CRA's website, in 2010 to 2011, 834 audits were performed as part of the program, which resulted in the "identification" of approximately $87 million dollars. The website does not provide details as to how much of that money was actually collected.

It is important to understand that the CRA conducts two general types of audits — criminal and regulatory. The regulatory audits may turn into criminal audits if the auditor suspects tax evasion or criminal activity. It is equally important to know that when the audit becomes criminal in nature, a taxpayer has certain rights under the Canadian Charter of Rights and Freedoms. As such, it is always important during each point in an audit to know whether the auditor has some sort of suspicion which could cause him or her to collect information for the purpose of a criminal investigation. If this becomes the case, a taxpayer is well advised to contact a tax lawyer.

1.12 Informant tips

Canadian tax laws are not to be taken lightly by taxpayers. The CRA views noncompliance seriously and has set up many measures to ensure taxpayers to not abuse the tax system. For instance, one who suspects a taxpayer of tax evasion may contact the Informant Leads Centre online or via the 1-800 numbers, and when doing so, the identity of the informant need not be disclosed. Informants may be concerned citizens, but a great many others come from estranged business partners, disgruntled ex-spouses, and vindictive third parties. Informant provided leads are then directed to the Informant Leads Program, where information is coordinated and reviewed to determine if any noncompliance exists. If there is evidence of noncompliance, enforcement action may occur.

At present, the information leads received are far more numerous than the CRA's ability to audit. So fear not: if you suspect that somebody has already snitched on you or will do so in the future, and you have not yet heard from the CRA regarding a possible audit, you may still have time to come forward through the Voluntary Disclosures Program, and get away without any criminal charges or penalties. (See Chapter 10 for further details on the program.)

The CRA is attempting to establish a system to more effectively minimize noncompliance based on informant leads. So, it can be expected that over time, the CRA will have developed a strategy to catch up on the leads that come in.

1.13 Prior audits

Taxpayers who have been subjected to a prior audit are not immune to the CRA ensuring future compliance for the same issue. Many times the CRA will perform audits to follow up on previous mistakes or transgressions — especially when there is a high risk of the taxpayer repeating an offense.

1.14 Being self-employed or running a business

For reasons discussed earlier, the CRA enjoys auditing businesses and the self-employed. They are the ones who have the highest risk of tax loss. Technology has made it easy for the CRA to carry out random audits or targeted investigations of these taxpayers. Investigators can select returns that are above or below average in a specific financial category or it can combine various financial factors in one search. For example, one year the CRA audited all pharmacists with less-than-average profits and found many cases of noncompliance, some of which were taken to court.

Since small-business audits are where the CRA tends to find most of its lost taxes, it is not surprising that the amount of audits has increased by 10 to 15 percent with respect to both small- and medium-sized businesses within the past few years. Increases in the number of audits has also been noticed by the Canadian Federation of Business, which indicates that of its small-business members, the percentage of audits has increased from 16 to 21 percent in just four years.

1.15 Discrepancies between GST or HST returns and income tax returns

The CRA — and anybody capable of fifth grade math — can determine whether an individual has reported enough income to justify his or her GST or HST returns, and whether the person has reported enough GST or HST for the amount of income he or she has reported. If these two returns do not match, a taxpayer will be audited. Remember, a taxpayer is also required to report his or her revenue on both types of returns. This makes it incredibly easy to connect the dots even without fifth grade math.

1.16 Rental income

A taxpayer with rental income should be careful to claim the appropriate carrying and operating costs and declare any income.

If a property is rented to a taxpayer, it is fairly easy to determine if the taxpayer is living in a basement apartment because he or she will have the same address as another taxpayer. By this same reasoning, it is also easy for the CRA to find taxpayers who are lying about their marital status — they claim single but have the same address. Sometimes even roommates are wrongly declared by the CRA to be living in a common-law relationship and reassessed accordingly.

The CRA can determine which taxpayers are renting homes and apartments, and which taxpayers own the property. One way or another, the CRA often finds out about undeclared rental income from information provided by the tenant and other third parties. Even if a taxpayer declares all rental income, he or she is still subject to being audited since the CRA knows that taxpayers often overstate the expenses associated with renting a property — particularly if he or she rents part of his or her home.

1.17 Shareholder loans

Some corporations legitimately lend money to their shareholders, which is paid back over time. However, in many cases, taxpayers attempt to avoid or delay taxation by claiming that monies received from a corporation throughout the tax year were loans by the corporation to them as shareholders, and not income actually earned by the taxpayers.

When the CRA sees loans being regularly made to shareholders of a company — especially when previous loans have not yet been repaid — the CRA becomes very suspicious, and it is likely to investigate.

If you are considering obtaining loans from your corporation, you are well advised to seek the expertise of a good accountant prior to doing so.

1.18 Errors and missing information

When obvious errors are present in a tax return, the CRA frequently fixes the errors and alerts the taxpayer to the fact that he or she has been assessed. Other times, when there are errors or pieces of missing information, the CRA may choose to audit. As such, it is best to ensure that your returns are prepared properly by a well-qualified accountant or income tax preparer. The level of expertise of the individual chosen should match to the level of complexity of your return.

1.19 Employment expenses

Since very few employees are actually permitted to claim employment expenses (e.g., employees who work partially on commission), claiming expenses, particularly the first time, can lead to an audit.

1.20 Investment gains and losses

The CRA likes to audit investment gains and losses since many taxpayers do not correctly identify their gains as income tax and instead choose to characterize their gains as capital gains, which have a favourable tax treatment. Further, when large losses are applied to offset tax payable, the CRA is particularly interested and may likely audit the taxpayer's return.

2. How the CRA Reviews Your Tax Return

The CRA maintains four different review programs which function to verify the figures on taxpayers' returns. Each of the income tax returns filed is electronically analyzed, and based on this analysis, certain returns where there is a high risk of tax loss, are referred for review. Other members of the reviewed groups are selected randomly. To accomplish the review, the CRA makes requests for specific documentation or receipts from the taxpayer.

2.1 Pre-assessment review program

The pre-assessment review program is a pre-assessment tax audit. Both high risk returns and returns at random are analyzed electronically by the CRA. It reviews credits and deductions, and may contact the taxpayer by mail allowing for the taxpayer to make necessary adjustments or corrections prior to the CRA issuing a Notice of Assessment.

2.2 Processing review program

The next review program is the processing review program and only occurs once a Notice of Assessment has been issued. In this program, the CRA looks to ensure that the taxpayer has claimed deductions accurately, and appropriately, and looks to verify whether the taxpayer has the necessary paperwork to substantiate the claim. If an error is uncovered, the CRA will issue a new Notice of Assessment, otherwise it will issue a letter indicating that there is no adjustment required.

2.3 Matching program

The third review program concerns information slips provided by third parties, or the matching program. The CRA cross-references all returns to these information slips, and ensures that they match. It looks to see that all relevant information from third parties (e.g., financial institutions and employers) has been declared on a taxpayer's return. If a discrepancy is found, the taxpayer is notified and requested to produce documentation to the CRA for clarification. If an adjustment is required, the CRA will issue a new Notice of Assessment.

The matching program is used to compare the information concerning the return with information it has received from third parties. The CRA cross-references spouses' returns to make sure that important information matches. When it finds one or more discrepancies, it calculates the amount of income tax that is potentially recoverable should a reassessment be issued.

2.4 RRSP excess contribution review program

This program ensures that taxpayers have completed the correct Individual Tax Return for RRSP Excess Contributions (T1-OVP) and ensures that taxpayers' records with respect to their RRSPs are correct. Taxpayers who are determined to potentially have excess RRSP contributions are contacted by the CRA in order to review their situation and take appropriate measures to correct it.

3. CRA Special Projects

In attempt to recover as many lost tax dollars as possible, the CRA routinely embarks on special projects. As computer technology has improved, in conjunction with an increase in electronically filed personal and corporate tax returns, the CRA's capabilities with respect to these special projects have become much more formidable. The CRA's broad authority to require companies to provide information regarding unnamed third parties has been upheld by Canadian courts, including the Supreme Court. Already the CRA has made requests of information from such third parties as the Montreal Real Estate Board, eBay, and Amex so that their clients could be investigated for tax fraud. One can expect going forward that none of the CRA's dealings with companies are going to be private. If the CRA wants to get its hands on the information, it likely will.

6
WHAT TO EXPECT IF YOU ARE AUDITED

In Information Circular 71-14R3, the Canada Revenue Agency (CRA) describes the purpose of the tax audit as follows:

"While there is, in Canada, a high standard of public compliance with the law, a self-assessment tax system can be maintained only through vigilant and continuous inspection of returns. The primary purpose of the tax audit is to monitor and maintain the self-assessment system. As such, it plays an important role in the achievement of the objectives of the Department which are to collect the taxes imposed by law through the encouragement of voluntary compliance and to maintain public confidence in the integrity of the tax system."

Canadian taxpayers, rightly so, panic when they find out they are going to be audited — regardless of how careful they have been with their filings. It is important if you are going through an audit that you understand your rights and obligations as a Canadian taxpayer, which could save you thousands of dollars. (See Chapter 1 to review taxpayers' rights and obligations.)

1. The Audit Process

The audit process can be terrifying for many Canadian taxpayers because it leaves them feeling vulnerable. Having some knowledge about the process of being audited and knowing your rights can be empowering. The audit process is adversarial, meaning characterized by opposition or conflict. The taxpayer is in a conflicting position with the auditor, whose job it is to find hidden tax dollars that may be assessed against a taxpayer.

The best way to address the vulnerability is to understand the audit process and your rights as a taxpayer, including the right to have a representative, such as a tax lawyer, deal with the audit on your behalf. Note that hiring a lawyer or other representative does not indicate to the CRA that you're guilty of fraud. It is an indication that you want the process to go smoothly as much as it is an indication that the CRA will not be permitted to intimidate you or violate any of your rights.

1.1 Step 1: The audit letter

The audit process commences when the CRA issues a letter to the taxpayer which indicates that he or she has been selected for an audit. In this letter the CRA provides an entire laundry list of what documents it expects the taxpayer to make available for inspection. A particular issue or area of concern may be outlined, such as the purchase and sale of a property, or the CRA may simply want to see everything.

Typically, the CRA expects the taxpayer to make available for inspection all books, records, important contracts, invoices, minute books, and any other documents which would be required to justify a taxpayer's claims on his or her return for the year or years under audit. Further, the letter asks the taxpayer to arrange a suitable time and date for an initial meeting.

With individuals and small corporations, the CRA is permitted to reassess returns for three years from the original date of assessment and filing. For large corporations this period may extend to four years. In the case where the CRA suspects and can establish negligence or fraud, it has no limit of time.

It is important when the CRA sends the initial audit letter to determine whether it has the right to audit the years in question. Sometimes (although very rarely) an auditor will send an initial letter which asks the taxpayer to make available documents and records for a year which according to law, the CRA is not permitted to audit. Such a year is technically referred to by tax professionals and the CRA as being "statute-barred" — the statute (the *Income Tax Act* or the *Excise Tax Act*) does not permit the CRA to audit a year that far in the past. Other times an auditor will commence an audit of a particular year, but will fail to file the reassessment in time. In these cases, the reassessment should be thrown out, and on occasion, an auditor sneakily requests that a taxpayer sign a waiver in order to permit a reassessment outside of the regular time limits. Whenever such a waiver is presented to a taxpayer, he or she should speak to a lawyer to determine whether or not he or she should sign it. Some other waivers are even used by the CRA to prevent a taxpayer from taking a matter to court if he or she disagrees with the CRA's findings. All waivers should be initially treated with suspicion and should not be signed unless the taxpayer's lawyer has advised him or her to sign it.

In cases where the audit is not commenced with an informal letter, they are sometimes commenced with a formal "requirement" for information, which will cite a relevant section of the *Income Tax Act* (ITA) which requires you to legally comply with the request. Such a requirement will provide particulars of the documents or information that must be produced, and it should include a warning that failure to comply may result in prosecution. It will also have a deadline. If a taxpayer is unsure whether or not to comply, he or she should speak to a tax lawyer.

1.2 Step 2: The audit — information gathering and analysis

The audit will typically take place at your home if you are an individual, or your office if you are a corporation or a self-employed individual. During the audit process, the auditor may examine your premises or your home office, and he or she may examine all the books and records that he or she has requested in the initial letter. Small audits are typically completed fairly quickly, with a meeting of only a few hours, which may or may not result in the auditor copying a few documents and leaving to his or her office to complete the investigation. Other audits may take days or weeks of on-site meetings and questions, and the exchange of documents can sometimes take months when documents from third parties need to be requested because the taxpayer doesn't have them readily available.

One important thing to consider when speaking to an auditor is that he or she is only entitled to information that is relevant to his or her job in auditing a taxpayer's returns. Any casual conversation with the auditor should be avoided because he or she may be attempting to obtain information to which he or she would not be otherwise entitled.

Another item of equal importance is that a taxpayer must try his or her best to prevent auditors from walking away with his or her original documents or receipts. I have had numerous clients who were audited and who were not able to properly fight the outcome of the audit because auditors had taken and misplaced original documents and, in other cases, where original documents were lost in the mail between the client and the auditor.

According to Canadian tax laws (and some Canadian business laws), all taxpayers are required to keep their records, including physical and electronically stored documents, and upon request, a taxpayer should be able to produce them for inspection. As such, they must either be kept in Canada or be made available in Canada on short notice.

A taxpayer is under a legal obligation during an audit to provide the auditor with any relevant information or documents which will help the auditor determine the tax owing for the period being audited, and generally an auditor will provide a standard checklist of all the documents that he or she intends to review during the course of the audit. Items such as bank statements, invoices, contracts, insurance policies, credit card statements, and a host of other documents are generally included in such a checklist and must be produced to the auditor upon request.

A taxpayer may be asked to substantiate some or all of his or her expenses, and among the records that a taxpayer must keep and be able to produce for the CRA are receipts and any other documentation including contracts, invoices, and cancelled cheques which relate to his or her business expenditures. Oftentimes, if a receipt is missing and the CRA cannot validate an expense, from experience I have seen that the auditor does not generally tend to accept secondary information to prove that the expenditure occurred, such as affidavits, credit card statements, invoices, contracts, etc., and the auditor will usually deny the expense. But sometimes enough secondary information can convince an auditor of an expense's legitimacy, and oftentimes this secondary information is sufficient for an Appeals Officer or a judge in the Tax Court of Canada. What is frustrating is that the CRA will sometimes have a receipt provided, yet it may still deny the claim if it does not have sufficient evidence to support that the receipt is genuine and was actually paid by the taxpayer. The best thing for a taxpayer is to keep a receipt and all relevant proof that he or she paid the amount in question.

Taxpayers should be aware that the CRA also performs criminal investigations of tax-related fraud. In these types of investigations, different rules may apply, and individuals may avail themselves of their rights under the

Canadian Charter of Rights and Freedoms. If a taxpayer determines or suspects that he or she is the subject of a criminal investigation, or an investigation could result in the discovery of information which may incriminate him or her, the taxpayer should contact a lawyer immediately to discuss the case.

As the onus is on the taxpayer to prove that he or she has accurately reported all his or her income and expenses, good record keeping is essential. Without it, the CRA auditor will likely make a determination of taxes owed without the benefit of complete information. Further, in certain cases, a taxpayer may be penalized or prosecuted for failure to keep proper records. (For further information on the types of records to keep and the length of time for which you should keep them, please review Chapter 2.)

1.3 Step 3: The proposal letter

Once the examination of documents is completed, and the auditor has determined his or her position with respect to the returns in question, the auditor will issue a letter to the taxpayer called the "Proposal Letter." The letter more or less reads: "Dear Taxpayer, we have completed our audit of your return, and we propose to make the following changes to your tax return." The remainder of the letter provides all the various details of the proposed changes, and certain explanations for the auditor's position. The auditor then outlines what the numbers looked like as filed, and what the numbers will look like if reassessed according to the proposal. Additionally, the auditor indicates whether he or she is considering the application of penalties onto the amounts in question. The auditor provides a 30-day window in which to provide all relevant documentation to prove him or her wrong.

In my experience, I have found that auditors do not like to be proved wrong, especially those auditors who come into an audit with a negative opinion of the taxpayer. If their hypothesis is that the taxpayer has undisclosed income and should not be able to afford the Porsche in his or her driveway, they will insist on perfect documentation before walking away and having their hypothesis fail. In fact, I have seen instances where individuals have received money or inheritances from family members overseas, have either moved into a better home, or paid off their mortgage, and were not able to produce proper documentation sufficient to convince an auditor of the money's origin. In these cases the auditor has always attempted to declare these funds as "undeclared income," which in turn means that the taxpayer must pay tax on amounts which otherwise would not have been taxable.

If a taxpayer produces further relevant documentation within the 30-day window, the auditor will consider it, and may change his or her position with respect to the initial proposal. Either way, unless the taxpayer's documentation is impeccable, and his or her accounting was perfect, he or she is likely to receive a reassessment after the auditor's review of the new materials. If a taxpayer chooses not to respond to the auditor within the 30 days allotted, or if he or she responds late, the auditor will simply reassess as per the proposal.

Prior to making the reassessment, the auditor prepares an Audit Report (T20), providing details as to the reasons for the reassessment. Once the audit report is reviewed and approved by the auditor's team leader, a reassessment is issued.

1.4 Step 4: The reassessment

Once the auditor has arrived at his or her final position, he or she will issue a reassessment. Once issued, this reassessment takes the place of any previous assessment or reassessment for the return in question, and its contents become fact if left unchallenged. This new reassessment will outline what is owed for the period in question. (See Chapter 9 for more information about objecting to an assessment or reassessment.)

2. What the CRA Can Do During an Audit

In order to be prepared for an audit and to get out of it relatively unscathed, it is important to understand the very broad powers of the CRA which allow it to demand or even seize documents (i.e., physical or electronic) both in your possession and in the possession of others (e.g., your accountant). Any information which can be used against you in order to prove that you were not declaring the correct amount of tax owing can be demanded by the CRA, and it can require under pain of punishment, that those demands are respected. Rest assured, any information which the CRA obtains will be used to ensure that you pay as much tax as possible.

Under Canadian tax law, the auditor is provided with the following rights:

- To examine all books, records, and documents of the taxpayer that could relate to the audit, and any books records and documents held by third parties, which pertain to the audit of the taxpayer.

- To enter and inspect home offices and any other place where the taxpayer carries out his or her business, holds property, or maintains records.

- To require cooperation of the taxpayer and third parties.

- To make a copy of any document required for the purpose of the audit (i.e., digital or physical) or to demand a printout of a digital document.

- To not to be interfered with. Section 231.5 of the act states that "no person shall, physically or otherwise, interfere with, hinder, or molest" an auditor while he or she is performing his or her duties.

2.1 Requirement for information

When an auditor issues a "requirement for information" letter, recipients of the letter are generally required to provide the information or document requested, and failure to comply with the terms of the letter can result in prosecution of the recipient, who may be the taxpayer or a third-party. If the taxpayer does not wish to provide the information being requested, he or she should speak to a lawyer before the deadline. Failure to do so could result in criminal prosecution and a trial.

If the request for information relates to the enforcement of Canadian tax law, courts will generally view the request as being valid, so a challenge in court had better be founded on solid ground. Further, the Supreme Court of Canada has protected the right to inspect and seize documents, which is explained in the case of R. v. McKinlay Transport Ltd., [1990] 1 S.C.R. 627:

"The *Income Tax Act*" is essentially a regulatory statute which controls the manner in which income tax is calculated and collected. It is based on the principle of self-reporting and self-assessment. To ensure compliance with the Act, the Minister of National Revenue must be given broad powers to audit taxpayers' returns and inspect all relevant records whether or not he has reasonable grounds for believing that a particular taxpayer has breached the Act. The integrity of the tax system can be maintained only by a system of random monitoring and s. 231(3) provides the least intrusive means by which effective monitoring of compliance with the Act can be effected. A taxpayer's expectation of privacy … *vis-à-vis* the Minister is relatively low. The taxpayer's privacy interest is protected as much as possible by s. 241 of the Act which forbids the disclosure of the taxpayer's records or the information contained therein to other persons or agencies. Therefore, the seizure contemplated by s. 231(3) is reasonable and does not infringe s. 8 of the *Charter*."

The Supreme Court went on to discuss the standard of reasonability with respect to a seizure of documents and indicated the following:

"The standard of review of what is 'reasonable' in a given context must be flexible if it is to be realistic and meaningful. It is consistent with this approach to draw a distinction between seizures in the criminal or quasi-criminal context to which the full rigours of the *Hunter* criteria will apply, and seizures in the administrative or regulatory context to which a lesser standard may apply depending upon the legislative scheme under review. In light of the regulatory nature of the legislation and the scheme enacted, it was evident in this case that the *Hunter* criteria were ill-suited to determine whether a seizure under s. 231(3) of the Act was reasonable."

3. Types of Audits

The following sections describe the different types of audits.

3.1 Correspondence audit

The simplest type of audit is a correspondence audit, and in most cases if you are self-employed or run a business, there is a very low likelihood that you will be audited in this category.

The name of the audit comes from the method by which the audit is completed — by correspondence. In this type of an audit, reserved for very simple tax returns, the taxpayer receives correspondence from the CRA which requests that the taxpayer provide certain documentation in order to verify amounts on his or her return. In this type of an audit, the taxpayer can expect to be asked for receipts, cancelled cheques, and certain other materials.

3.2 Office audit

Another way the CRA may perform an audit is by way of an office audit, which is a tax audit that takes place in the CRA office. In this type of audit the CRA agent will contact the individual or business being audited to request that the taxpayer provide the information that the auditor needs in order to conduct the audit to the office of the CRA.

The taxpayer is notified of this type of audit by mail. In the letter, specific items from the taxpayer's return are identified and the auditor requests that the documents in question are brought (or sent) to the auditor's office in order to be examined. While not quite as simple as a correspondence audit, the office audit is typically reserved for small businesses and self-employed individuals with sales of less than $500,000.

3.3 Field audit

The most common type of tax audit is a field audit, where one or more CRA agents inspect and scrutinize the financial records of the taxpayer, typically in his or her own place of business or residence. This type of audit obtains its name because it is conducted in the "field" as opposed to the auditor's office. Most incorporated businesses and partnerships are audited in this manner.

The CRA agent will contact the individual undergoing the tax audit to set up a date and time for the audit. Prior to the meeting, the CRA auditor will examine the taxpayer's file to become familiar with the case. The file will include the current tax filing under scrutiny and may include such information as past tax audits and financial statements. Based on this preparation, the auditor will go into the meeting with a list of questions for the taxpayer. The expert advice of a tax lawyer is particularly important to advise the taxpayer on the specific questions he or she should or should not answer or are legally required to answer in order to prevent damaging or self-incriminating statements from being made as well as to prevent any infringement of taxpayer rights by the CRA agent.

At commencement of the meeting, the CRA auditor will identify himself or herself with the official CRA identification card. The tax auditor may then attempt to speak with the taxpayer rather informally to get more information about the taxpayer and/or the business or industry he or she is in. The auditor may also want to take a tour of the place of business. Again, the assistance of a tax lawyer is crucial to help assess whether or not these requests are legal or to the best interest of the taxpayer.

The auditor will then begin with the analysis of the taxpayer's financial records. How deep the auditor will dig into the taxpayer's financial records is essentially up to the auditor and his or her supervisor. The CRA auditor may ask to examine bank account statements, invoices, journals, expense accounts, product inventory, sales contracts, appointment books, meeting minutes, shipping and receiving records, investments, etc. The tax auditor may also ask to speak with employees of the taxpayer. It is important to reiterate the benefits of legal representation at this stage of the auditing process, since a tax lawyer will defend your rights and represent taxpayer interests, unlike the auditor

who is there solely to represent his or her own interests as well as those of the CRA.

If the CRA agent decides that the information provided is inadequate or does not sufficiently explain the standard of living of the taxpayer, he or she may then have net worth statements drawn up to establish or confirm the taxpayer's income. According to the CRA, this is done "in a small minority of cases."

The CRA agent will normally save his or her queries for the end of the examination and will not question each individual item. At the tax audit's conclusion, the auditor will then decide whether a readjustment to the taxpayer's return is necessary. If it is, the taxpayer may request the proposed adjustments be put in writing for him or her or his or her tax lawyer's evaluation of these proposed changes, unless the taxpayer agrees with the auditor, in which case no proposal is drawn up and the CRA agent continues with the reassessment, where a Notice of Assessment or notice of reassessment is issued. If the auditor determines that the tax filing was accurate and there is no need for a readjustment, then the taxpayer and his or her representative will be informed.

3.4 Lifestyle (net worth) audit

If a taxpayer's books and records are inaccurate or sloppy, or if an auditor is having a difficult time obtaining all the necessary documents in order to perform the audit, he or she can undertake to perform a net worth audit and will examine the lifestyle of the taxpayer and his or her family. In this audit, the auditor is typically after proof that a taxpayer's lifestyle is more expensive than he or she would be able to afford, given the amounts the person declared on his or her returns. These types of audits are sometimes the most destructive — especially if the taxpayer's income appears to be insufficient to justify his or her lifestyle.

I have had numerous clients who have been audited in this manner, and many of them have had infusions of extra money from their family in order to support their lifestyle. In one particular case, I had a client who drove a Ferrari and lived in a million-dollar home, yet only declared earnings of approximately $40,000 per year. The auditor was relentless, and tried in every way possible to show that my client was not declaring the entire income. In this case, we had to provide affidavits and financial records from the taxpayer's family in order to prove the source of the extra money.

While performing a lifestyle or net worth audit, the auditor uses Statistics Canada data to determine a given standard of living, and how much a particular size of family requires in order to live that lifestyle. The auditor will add to these living expenses, the cost of the vehicles that the taxpayer drives, and the cost of any trips, private school tuitions, and other costs that he or she can establish the taxpayer pays to determine if the taxpayer can afford to pay all these costs based on the declared income. The auditor will then compare the amount of money and assets that a taxpayer had at the beginning of the audit period with the money and assets the taxpayer has at the end of the audit period to determine whether he or she was cheating on the return.

For example, a family of four may require $60,000 per year to live a certain lifestyle. If the auditor determines that at the beginning of a three-year audit period the family had $500,000 worth of property, cash, and vehicles, and at the end of the three-year period, had $700,000 of assets, he or she makes the following calculation:

The difference between the starting and ending assets are $200,000. Plus it would have cost the taxpayer $60,000 per year times three

years (or $180,000) in order to pay the expenses. So, if the taxpayer has $200,000 more assets, and spent $180,000 during the three-year period, it would appear as though he or she had earned $380,000 during that time. If the taxpayer declared only $70,000 per year, there would be a discrepancy of $380,000 to $210,000, or $170,000, which would have to be explained by the taxpayer, failing which he or she would be on the hook for unpaid taxes on $170,000 of undeclared income.

A few years ago I represented a taxpayer in a particularly unfair lifestyle audit. The subject of this particular audit was an immigrant family with six children. Since the family had six children and lived in Toronto, the auditor consulted the Statistics Canada data which indicated that for a family of that size in Toronto, they would have to generate an income of more than $100,000 per year in order to live. My client, however, only earned about $50,000 per year, and earned far less in some years. The auditor simply did not believe that the family could actually survive on the amount declared in the income tax return, and reassessed my client based on an assumed income of $100,000 per year. The results of the audit were so bad that the amount of taxes owed (about $40,000 per year) were approximately the amount of income earned for the entire year. There was no way that my client could afford to pay $40,000 of taxes when the family earnings were little more than that.

In order to prove the taxpayer's case, we had to show that unlike most families with six children, they only had two rooms for all the children — a boy's room and a girl's room. Further, we had to show that the family cooked all their own meals at home, and since they were vegetarian, they did not have to buy expensive meats and poultry. Unlike most families of eight, this family was able to survive in Toronto on $50,000 per year — sometimes with the assistance of a food bank for additional food.

When the CRA completes a net worth audit, it is assumed that it is correct. In this case, as in many other cases, the onus is on the taxpayer to prove the CRA wrong, which can be very difficult — especially when the auditor has a preconceived notion due to fancy vehicles in the driveway and a low income.

If the taxpayer disagrees with the findings on the audit, he or she has the ability to file an objection, and following an unsuccessful objection, can apply to the Tax Court of Canada to dispute the audit findings.

4. Preparing for an Audit

The key to being audited without losing your shirt is to be prepared. The better your record keeping is, the more likely you will be able to justify your expenses to the CRA auditor and avoid huge reassessments and penalties.

Keep in mind that when the day comes to be audited, and when an auditor arrives at your home or workplace, although he or she will be polite and friendly, he or she will be relentless in his or her quest to deny your expenses and charge you extra taxes. In order to do so, the auditor will attempt to reject expenses when original receipts, invoices, and mileage records are unavailable. Although there is no requirement under the law to produce originals, the auditors often deny expenses on this basis alone. To the auditor, a credit card statement is not an acceptable form of proof.

When preparing for an audit — either an actual audit that is upcoming, or a hypothetical audit that may or may not be in your future — a prepared taxpayer should keep in mind that auditors frequently choose to examine various areas in detail. Some of these areas are discussed in the sections below.

4.1 Business use of a vehicle

If you use a vehicle for both business and personal purposes, it is important that you can prove that the vehicle was in fact used for business purposes. More importantly, it is essential that you are able to prove exactly how much the vehicle was used for business purposes.

In order to keep track of the usage of a vehicle and justify expenses, it is best to keep a logbook in each one of your vehicles. An electronic logbook is also acceptable, thus allowing notes to be taken on smartphones. Not only is a logbook the best means to track a vehicle's use for tax purposes, it is also the form of proof that the CRA will be asking you to provide in the course of an audit. What the CRA will be looking for is the following for each day of use (if a vehicle is used exclusively for business purposes all day), and for each trip taken (if a vehicle is used for both business and personal purposes):

- Starting odometer reading
- Name of the person or company you visited
- Name of the place you went to purchase supplies and materials for your business
- Where you started your trip
- Where you finished your trip
- Each time you fill up the vehicle with gas. The CRA will sometimes perform an analysis of the amount of gas you would have consumed, given the type of vehicle driven and the fuel consumption of a vehicle of that type. Take note of the number of litres purchased, the price per litre, and the name of the gas station.

Since the CRA will allow a taxpayer to claim a percentage of repairs and other costs associated with maintaining the vehicle in relation to the percentage of the kilometres used for business purposes, it is important to be able to provide the auditor with both the total kilometres driven per year and the total number of kilometres driven for business. For example, if a taxpayer can prove with his or her logbook that he or she drove 20,000 kilometres in a year, 15,000 of which were for business use, he or she would be able to justify to an auditor that his or her claim of 75 percent of vehicle expenses was legitimate.

If you are being audited and do not have a logbook for the time periods in question, there are other ways to prove your use of the vehicle. With a certain degree of proof and information, a taxpayer can usually obtain some credit for vehicle expenses without a logbook.

Although many auditors may not find it acceptable, they may be able to be convinced by providing a current log as a representation of a typical month. If there is no current log, you may be able to reconstruct to a certain extent, a log of a recent month. This is typically done by working backwards from the current odometer reading, and making an entry for each appointment, meeting, and sales call that you have in your calendar. If you know the location of each of these meetings and sales calls, and their starting points, you would be able to calculate the driving distance between the points using Google so it would be no problem to record the distance in the log. By this same method, if you had detailed records of where you drove, for which appointments, and when, during the relevant period in question, you may be able to give fairly accurate records to the auditor.

Since odometer readings are taken into account for up to three years, they would be hard to obtain from memory, so you may want to consult service records. Every time a vehicle is serviced or has its oil changed, the odometer reading is recorded. Service records can be very useful when it comes time to requiring proof of odometer readings.

Beware: If you use your vehicle for both business and personal uses, or if a business claims that it has exclusive use of a vehicle for business purposes, sometimes the CRA auditor will look to the insurance policy as a means by which to show that the vehicle was not used for business. If the policy does not show that the vehicle is to be used for business purposes — other than commuting to and from work — the auditor may choose to use this as a means by which to deny or reduce your claim. That is not to say that this is always the case, but I have seen it happen. If an auditor attempts to use your insurance policy against you in order to deny your vehicle expenses, it is best to challenge the CRA — either personally or through a representative such as a tax lawyer.

4.2 Meals and entertainment

Meals and entertainment are always high up on the CRA's list of items to be examined due to the way in which they are abused. In terms of abuse, I would say that most people who are self-employed, or who own a small business improperly try to claim a number of receipts for personal meals and entertainment as business expenses. For some people it is a dinner here and a pair of hockey tickets there — nothing major. However, some people believe that running a business provides them with the ability to write off a large number of personal meals. Still, other people don't understand the rules, and inadvertently have inflated expense claims.

If you take a client for dinner, you can only claim 50 percent of the meal as an expense. You cannot claim your portion of the meal. There are certain exceptions to this rule, such as when you have to work out of town, depending on how far away you are, your meals may be covered. If you are going to claim a deduction for meals or entertainment, it is best to be informed before you file your return. In order to prove your case to the auditor, you should be prepared to hand over all receipts for meals and entertainment, with notes on the back indicating who was invited, and the reason.

4.3 Business use of the home

The situations that cause taxpayers to get into trouble with respect to claiming business use of their home is when they do not have the ability to prove its use, or they have claimed an amount that is far too high.

During an audit, in order to support a claim, you must be able to prove a number of things, most importantly, the parts of your home used for business expenses and the square-footage occupied by those parts. You may have to justify your need to use so much space, and prove that you use the space in the way that you claim. This means that the auditor may ask to visit your home to inspect how it is used for business. Further, you must be able to prove the total square-footage of your home and provide all relevant documentation to show your carrying costs (e.g., property tax bills, mortgage statements, and electricity bills).

Audits of business use of a home become particularly complicated when the CRA chooses to audit a taxpayer for years in which he or she has lived in another residence. Since the person no longer has his or her home office, the taxpayer is left in the awkward position of not having the ability to prove the square-footage of the home office or any other

details that would be helpful in making his or her claim. It is advisable for taxpayers who plan to move, to document with photos and floor plans, the way in which they used their house for business purposes. These photos could be worth thousands!

4.4 Lost or missing records

Realistically, if you don't have records to support the claim you made on your tax return, you are going to have your claim denied. Similarly, if you have records but the CRA determines they are insufficient, your claim will be denied.

If your records are destroyed, such as in a flood or fire, you need to have evidence. Take pictures of the damage and keep police reports and clear details of what has been lost. You should also consider what you can do to reconstruct your records.

On a more serious note, section 238 makes it a criminal offence to fail to comply with section 230. You can be fined an amount between $1,000 and $25,000 and be imprisoned for up to one year for failure to keep adequate books and records. Under section 231.2, the Minister can also require you to provide a specific document or information and if you fail to comply, you can face prosecution by the CRA. It is more common for the CRA to send you a letter to sign requiring that you maintain better books and records in the future. It would be fair to assume that if you are sent such an agreement, you are more likely to be audited in the future to determine whether you have complied with the requirement.

7
HOW TO ACHIEVE THE BEST RESULTS FROM AN AUDIT

While the CRA claims that an important objective of audits is to uniformly interpret and apply the law, in reality, the situation is quite different. In actual fact, if one compared audits or auditors, one would see that the outcomes of audits have a great deal to do with the type or size of a business being audited, whether the taxpayer has representatives, or even the mood of the auditor on that particular day.

With respect to the size of a business being audited, the smaller the business, the less likely the CRA is likely to earn from the audit, and the easier it will be to find the discrepancies. As a result, in my experience, small businesses often receive poor-quality audits from junior auditors, who don't have enough experience to perform a quality audit, and have such a high caseload that they don't have the time to even perform a proper audit. These audits are often left unchallenged because these taxpayers can-

not afford to have proper representation to fight the CRA. However, big corporations usually have highly trained auditors assigned to their audits — auditors who are Chartered Accountants, and who are given enough time to do their job properly. Similarly, it is the large corporations who can more easily afford to have proper legal representation when the CRA makes an error, thus increasing the likelihood that they will achieve a fair outcome.

There is no guaranteed way to do well in an audit and prevent the CRA from reassessing a taxpayer for additional taxes owed, but if an audit is handled properly, taxpayers can reduce their taxes owing, and they may be able to avoid penalties. In many cases, if they have the correct documentation, the taxpayers can obtain positive results without any representation. However, sometimes when the taxpayers have something to hide, or when they have been sloppy with their record keeping — especially when the discrepancy is more than $100,000 — they are best to seek legal advice before proceeding with the audit.

1. Know Your Rights

Where there are discrepancies, intentional or not, large enough that the CRA could possibly conduct a criminal investigation as a result, a taxpayer must be even more careful. While auditors are required to refer files to criminal investigations once they have sufficient proof to suggest that the taxpayer may be guilty of a criminal tax offense, they often delay the referral and without the taxpayer's knowledge, continue to collect information which could be used to prosecute the taxpayer criminally.

Canadians have protection under the Canadian Charter of Rights and Freedoms (Charter) against self-incrimination (section 7) and against unreasonable search and seizure (section 8). Since under the *Income Tax Act* the CRA is able to conduct an audit and seize documents and materials from taxpayers without a warrant (which would be required by the police in order to gather the same evidence), the Supreme Court of Canada addressed the conflict in the decisions of R. v. Jarvis [2002] 3 S.C.R. 757 and R. v. Ling [2002] 3 S.C.R. 814. In these two decisions, the court put forth a "Predominant Purpose" test to determine whether a taxpayer must comply with the CRA in its enforcement of the *Income Tax Act*, or whether they can invoke their Charter rights and refuse to cooperate with the CRA.

Under this test, the Supreme Court notes that when the predominant purpose in acquiring information from the taxpayer becomes an investigation to determine criminal liability, the taxpayer may no longer be compelled to comply with the CRA's requests and requirements.

So it is important to know why an auditor is requesting a particular document and to understand your rights with respect to when you can refuse to comply.

2. Don't Withhold Requested Documents

In certain cases, clients decide to withhold certain requested documents, and nothing I can do will change their minds. Sometimes, I am led to suspect that these documents don't even exist. For certain lucky clients, the auditor is offered the easy way out, and instead of having to look at a bunch of documents in order to perform his or her audit, the auditor simply denies the expenses that could have been supported by the documents in question. In these cases, the auditor saves time, avoids paper cuts from sifting through the documents, and gets a big, fat reassessment which goes to his or her credit. The downside is that the taxpayer is left unable to claim his or her expenses and will pay more tax than he or she should.

3. Don't Provide Too Many Documents

Sometimes taxpayers believe that it is strategic to provide the auditor with way more than he or she has asked for, or to "burry them in paper." Sometimes this works and the auditor becomes bored or runs out of time. In these successful cases, the auditor typically looks at a representative sample of the documents and makes his or her decisions on that basis.

This tactic of too much information is ill-advised because some auditors will actually go through everything. I have heard of numerous cases where taxpayers have provided so much additional paperwork that the auditors were able to learn damaging information which otherwise they would never have had access.

4. Keep Informed by Reading Materials Published by the CRA

The CRA publishes a great deal of materials that can be helpful in understanding what may trigger an audit, and the way to achieve the best results is by helping avoid an audit from occurring in the first place.

There are numerous documents available on the CRA's website which can help a taxpayer determine areas of concern. Included in the materials with which taxpayers should familiarize themselves are newsletters, technical interpretations, and taxpayer alerts. Rather than keeping the reasons for an audit a mystery and surprising taxpayers, the CRA would prefer it if Canadians were informed about what may trigger an audit, which in turn may convince them to be more honest on their tax returns.

5. Audit Tips

The following are some additional audit tips:

- When you receive the request to set a date for the audit, take a look at the list of documents that the auditor wants to see and determine the earliest date you can provide them for inspection. Do not avoid calling the auditor because this will get the audit off to a bad start.

- Determine whether you need representation. Remember, having a representative help you through your audit is your right. It is not a sign of guilt, and when representatives handle audits on behalf of a taxpayer, oftentimes they can save the taxpayer many thousands of dollars more than their fees. In some audits I have saved taxpayers hundreds of thousands of dollars for a fraction of the fee. Besides saving money, it is often far less stressful to have a representative deal directly with the auditors.

- Avoid having conversations with the auditor which are irrelevant to the audit. These conversations could simply be a fishing expedition, and you may say the wrong thing. Keep the auditor on target and focused on the documents you have provided. Do answer questions which are relevant to the audit.

- If possible, arrange to have the audit done at your representative's office. This minimizes the opportunity for the auditor to snoop around and ask questions of your employees.

- Remember that the auditor does not have the final say and sometimes he or she is wrong! Once an audit is complete, you have or your representative has the opportunity to challenge the auditor's proposal prior to a reassessment, and after the reassessment the objection process is available. If a satisfactory result is not obtained during the objection, you can appeal to the Tax Court of Canada.

- An auditor only has a certain amount of time in order to reassess a taxpayer, and sometimes when he or she is getting close to the deadline, the auditor will try to get the taxpayer to sign a waiver allowing him or her to reassess outside of the regular period. Never sign a waiver before speaking to a tax lawyer. It may very well be a trick.

- If you suspect that the purpose of an auditor's request is to get evidence that could be used to prosecute you, you should call a tax lawyer immediately.

- Do not provide more documents than were requested. Ensure that the documents provided to the auditor are clear, organized, and on target. Keep all of the receipts neatly organized by month and year. When it comes time to preparing your tax return or if you are audited, the process will go more smoothly if you are organized, saving you time and money.

- If you use your vehicle for business and personal purposes, keep a mileage log of each time you use the vehicle for business. Take note of the starting mileage and the final mileage for each trip. Also take note of the price of gas at the time. If you make a claim for a deduction related to automobile expenses for your business, you will need this. Keep these logs for at least three years. Business may change, and you may need to be able to prove your vehicle expenses for any given year.

- If you use part of your home as an office for your business, make sure to measure the actual space used for business purposes and divide that by the total square footage of your home. You will be able to deduct a percentage of utilities, rent, mortgage interest, and other carrying costs. Also, be aware that large claims for home offices can be the cause of an audit. Don't get red-flagged. Be reasonable.

- If you want to donate to charity, donate directly to the charity and be sure to get the charitable receipt which you will need to claim the charitable contribution on your income tax return. Also be sure to keep a copy of the cheque that you used to make the donation. During an audit, the CRA often requires both the receipt and the cancelled cheque. If you don't have either one of these, your donation may be denied.

- Before you donate to any charity, ensure that the charity is registered in good standing with the CRA. Avoid donating to charity through some other organization. These programs are often schemes, and may cause you to be penalized and audited.

- You will not be able to rely on conversations you have had with the CRA over the phone or in person. These conversations including any erroneous advice provided to a taxpayer are not binding on the CRA. In cases where taxpayers relied on such advice which turned out to be incorrect, they will still be accountable for their taxes with any applicable interest and penalties. Where a taxpayer can prove that he or she relied on incorrect information from the CRA, he or she can file a complaint with the Taxpayers' Ombudsman and file a Request for Taxpayer Relief and cite the incorrect information as the grounds for the request. If successful, penalties and interest may be reduced. Record the name and extension of anybody at the CRA who has given you advice. You may need this.

- Always meet the deadlines provided by the auditor. If you cannot provide information in the required time, ask for an extension well ahead of time.

- If you have made a claim for employment expenses, you must be able to show the auditor a copy of your employment contract which says that you are responsible for certain expenses, and you must be able to produce a Declaration of Conditions of Employment (T2200).

- If the CRA treats you unfairly in the course of an audit, or violates one of your service-related rights from the Taxpayer Bill of Rights (see Chapter 17), you have the option to file a service-level complaint with the Taxpayers' Ombudsman, who reviews complaints and makes recommendations to the Minister of National Revenue.

- If you are receiving income from rental properties, you must be very careful to take the necessary steps to understand when you are making a capital improvement to your property versus routine maintenance and repairs. If these amounts are claimed incorrectly, this could spark an audit. It is best to get good accounting advice prior to filing these figures. Also, for each renovation project, it is best to keep invoices and receipts separate.

- If you are planning to move, be sure to get proof that you actually lived there. Any gains made from the sale of your principal residence are tax exempt, and if it comes time to proving that you actually lived in a property that you sold, be prepared to show that your bills were going there and, if possible, take photos showing furniture and personal effects. Also be sure to take photos of any spaces that you declare as a home office.

- The CRA routinely compares taxpayers who are in the same industry. Ensure that your expense structure is in line with similar types of businesses.

- Try to keep your returns fairly consistent from year-to-year. Big or odd changes could be cause for your return to be red-flagged for an audit.

- Make sure your returns are complete and accurate. Errors can trigger audits.

- Ensure that the proper tax return preparer is used. Some taxpayers have more complicated returns and require advice of a Chartered Accountant. It is best to err on the side of caution and hire somebody qualified to help you with your returns. The better the help, the better your returns are likely to be. This will help prevent an audit, and it will help you defend against an audit.

- If you have claimed expenses that you know you cannot support if you were to be audited, or if you have not declared income which would be found during an audit, you may come forward without prosecution or penalties through the Voluntary Disclosures Program (see Chapter 10). This is a far better outcome than an audit which would uncover the problem.

8
BUSINESS AUDITS

In general, the audit of a business is not very different from a personal audit. The auditor's job is to examine one or more returns and try to find areas where additional taxes can be assessed. While the business tax return can be audited, in general there are two main areas of concern to businesses and self-employed individuals: the Goods and Services Tax (GST) or Harmonized Sales Tax (HST) audits and payroll audits.

Given that GST or HST and payroll deductions are "trust" amounts, the Canada Revenue Agency (CRA) takes them even more seriously than it does income taxes. While the CRA used to perform complete, general audits, looking at both income tax and GST or HST, the approach has shifted to specialized audits where either income tax is being audited or trust amounts (i.e., GST, HST, or payroll).

1. Being Selected for a Business Audit

According to the CRA, the following sections outline the four common ways of selecting business returns for an audit.

1.1 Computer-generated lists

Computer-generated lists are the primary way of selecting a return for an audit. The CRA's computer system prepares lists after comparing financial information of taxpayers in the same industry or occupation. Where there is a potential for recovery of under declared revenues, the returns will be put on a list. From the list the CRA chooses specific returns for audit.

1.2 Audit projects

The CRA is constantly looking for certain groups of taxpayers who have a low level of compliance. If the agency finds a group, such as construction workers (who notoriously work under the table and don't declare all of their earnings), they may engage in a special audit projects of all construction workers on a local, regional, or national level.

1.3 Leads

There are two kinds of leads that may get a business audited. Information from outside sources, such as confidential informants who call the tips phone line, and internal information such as leads from audits or other investigations.

1.4 Secondary files

An audit can be brought about because of a relationship between the taxpayer and another taxpayer who is being or has been audited. In some cases, when one business has a partnership with another business, the nature of the partnership may cause it to be audited. In other circumstances, it may also be convenient to audit a parent company when one of its subsidiaries is being audited.

2. Types of Business Audits

The following sections outline the types of business audits.

2.1 Corporate tax audit

While a corporate tax audit is not very different from any other audit, certain documents are examined in the course of a corporate tax audit that are not typically looked at in other audits. These documents include the following:

- Financials including a general ledger and financial statements.
- Corporate documents including minute books and incorporation documents.
- Documents identifying related parties including parent, subsidiary, and affiliated corporations as well as major shareholders and directors.
- Legal agreements with partners, suppliers, clients, and related parties.
- Dividend statements.
- Loan balances.

2.2 GST and HST audits

Similar to other types of audits, GST and HST audits are performed both on a random basis, and on the basis of risk. Those returns with a higher risk of errors or omissions are selected for audit along with a random sample from all returns filed.

In order to properly defend against an audit, it is essential that all relevant books and records regarding GST or HST liabilities and input credits are readily available at the time of the audit. The requirement for businesses to keep records for the purposes of the GST or HST is found in section 286 of the *Excise Tax Act*. Such records must be kept if a taxpayer —

- carries on a business,
- engages in a commercial activity in Canada,
- is obligated to file a GST or HST return, or
- claims a GST or HST rebate or refund.

Things to consider before or during your GST or HST audit:

- Have you registered for the GST or HST (if required to do so)?
- Were you collecting the proper GST or HST amounts from the right customers or clients?
- Do you have all your receipts for your input tax credits?

2.3 Payroll audit

During the course of a payroll audit, the CRA is looking for two things:

- To ensure that the taxpayer has been withholding and remitting the correct payroll taxes.

- To ensure that all workers are properly designated as employees or contractors.

Sometimes a business will employ a worker as a contractor, but it will have no idea that this was incorrect until years later when audited. Sometimes the auditor will claim that workers are employees when they are not. Just because an auditor makes a certain claim does not mean that he or she is correct. Remember that the results of an audit can be challenged — firstly by responding to the proposal letter, and secondly by objecting to a reassessment that stems from the audit.

Consider the following before or during your payroll audit:

- Have you remitted all the necessary payroll deductions?

- Have you been withholding the correct amount for Employment Insurance (EI), Canadian Pension Plan (CPP), and income tax?

- Do you have proper documentation for all your employees? For example, do you have their addresses and Social Insurance Numbers?

- Do you have proper documentation for all contractors — either a business number or a Social Insurance Number?

- Have you properly considered whether you are justified in treating workers as contractors?

- Do you have the relevant contracts in place?

- Is there anything else you can do to increase the odds that the CRA will consider your works as contractors?

3. Avoiding Delays in a Business Audit

Many business audits are performed quickly and efficiently, while some of my clients have complained to me that their audits have taken many months to complete. The difference between a smooth and quick audit and one that drags on for what seems like an eternity can be as simple as the level of organization of the company.

Typically those companies with complete and organized books and ledgers experience audits that are smoother and faster than companies whose records are a mess. While the CRA's auditors may accept a shoebox of receipts from an individual who is being audited, their expectations are far greater when it comes to a business. When documents are missing, incomplete, or difficult to find, auditors are less than charitable, and may reassess the business taxpayer in the absence of certain documents. For example, if receipts which are required in order to substantiate expenses are either missing or difficult to find or read, the auditor may proceed as if the receipts did not exist at all. The auditor is not going to prepare financial ledgers and organize receipts for the taxpayer.

Whether your business has already been sent a notice for an audit or not, it is always best to keep all records and documents in order in a format that can easily be accessed should you be selected for an audit. For further information on record keeping, it is best to consult the CRA guide entitled "Keeping Records" (RC4409). It is available on the CRA's website at www.cra-arc.gc.ca/E/pub/tg/rc4409/README.html.

9
NOTICES OF ASSESSMENT, PENALTIES, AND INTEREST

After a taxpayer files a tax return, the Canada Revenue Agency (CRA) processes the return, and sends the taxpayer a Notice of Assessment which indicates how much tax the taxpayer owes. A Notice of Assessment is issued after GST and HST returns, personal income tax returns, and corporate tax returns are processed. If the taxpayer has filed the return on time and there are no errors found on the return, the amounts printed on the Notice of Assessment correspond exactly to the amounts provided by the taxpayer. However, when there are errors on the return, the CRA will change the figures, and in cases where the returns were not filed on time, or where the taxpayer made errors which according to the CRA, amounted to gross negligence, penalties are applied to the taxes owed. Furthermore, when the returns are filed late, interest charges are also imposed by the CRA and will show up on the Notice of Assessment.

In cases where the taxpayer has not filed the necessary returns, the CRA oftentimes will assess the taxpayer based on a worst-case-scenario and will send an appropriate Notice of Assessment. In these cases, the amount of tax assessed does not take into consideration credits which would normally be available to the taxpayer, and it is then up to the taxpayer to either file a correct return or dispute the figures provided by the CRA. In such "arbitrary" or "notional" assessments, as they are called, interest and penalty charges are also applied.

Notices of Reassessment are also issued once figures have been changed. Such reassessments may be issued after a taxpayer has filed his or her return and after the CRA has arbitrarily assessed them, and may also be issued after a taxpayer successfully disputes a previous Notice of Assessment, or after an audit where the CRA has shown that the figures listed on the previous Notice of Assessment were incorrect.

1. CRA Notices

The Notice of Assessment (T451) is issued by the CRA to every person who has filed an income tax return. The Notice of Reassessment (T491) is only issued following changes that were made to a taxpayer's return — either by the taxpayer or by the CRA following an audit.

The Notices of Assessment and Reassessment, which are for personal, corporate, and GST or HST returns, provide a number of pieces of information including the amount of taxes which must be paid or which will be refunded to the taxpayer. The following information is included in the notices:

- Refund or balance owed: The assessment informs you of whether you are to receive a refund or that you still have a balance owing.

- Corrections made by the CRA: If the CRA has made any corrections to your return, this information will be included on the assessment.

- Total household income: Line 150 of the tax return shows the total taxable income, which the CRA uses to determine eligibility for specific tax programs.

- RRSP deduction limit: This indicates the maximum amount that a taxpayer can contribute to his or her RRSP.

- Repayment for the Home Buyers' Plan (HBP): The amount you are required to repay in the current tax year is shown if you have benefited from a home-tax deduction and you have withdrawn money from your RRSP in order to participate in the HBP.

- Carry forward amounts for education: If you are a student who has not taken advantage of your entire student-tax deduction in order to reduce your taxes owing to zero, you are allowed to carry forward the unused portions for tuition, books, and education-related expenses. The unused portion is shown on the notice.

- Unused net capital losses: Unused net capital losses which can be applied to offset capital gains can be carried forward indefinitely or carried back three years are shown in the notice as well as the unused portion.

- Tax-Free Savings Account (TFSA): The TFSA contributions, withdrawals, and unused contributions are noted on the notice.

- Penalties and interest: All penalties that have been levied for the return in question will be shown on the notice, along with the interest applicable.

Since there is only a limited time in which to challenge a notice, you are advised to read your notice carefully, looking both for inaccuracies and details as to the limitation periods for filing an objection.

2. Objecting to the Assessment or Reassessment

If a taxpayer feels that an audit was unfair, or that the CRA is incorrect with respect to what is shown on a Notice of Assessment or reassessment, he or she has 90 days from the date of the assessment to file a Notice of Objection (T400A) with the CRA. Additionally, if the taxpayer misses the deadline, the CRA will routinely allow the person up to 12 months in order to obtain an extension in which to file the Notice of Objection. However, in many cases, the CRA has been known to be strict with businesses by denying them extensions.

During the objection, the CRA appoints an appeals officer to determine whether the taxpayer's position is correct. The process of appointing a CRA staff member to the case can take upwards of nine months, and the actual objection may take weeks or months to be determined by the appeals officer.

While the CRA is presumed to be correct if a taxpayer does not challenge it, and while the onus is on the taxpayer to establish that he or she has been incorrectly assessed, it is important to remember that the CRA can be, and very often is, wrong.

Irrespective of what the established CRA policy is, it may be breaking or misinterpreting the law, and irrespective of what you read in any CRA document or guide, there is still a chance that the CRA has made an error. If something seems unfair or incorrect, it is best to get advice from a knowledgeable tax accountant or tax lawyer.

Note that if an employee of the CRA gives you information in writing or over the phone, that person could also be incorrect. In short, be careful when you rely on information provided by the CRA. It is usually correct, but at times — especially when it concerns the amount of taxes it claims a taxpayer owes — it may be wrong, and the taxpayer may be well served in obtaining good advice from somebody who is not an employee of the CRA.

I have had clients who in the past have relied on incorrect information provided by CRA employees. In some cases, even though the taxpayers had documented who had provided the information and when, and some taxpayers had been provided with information in writing, they had not been able to use the fact that the CRA made an error to support their position.

They were generally told by the CRA that employee X made an error but that the error did not bind the CRA. However, a number of my clients were subsequently informed that they should apply for the relief of any interest or penalty amounts which they had been assessed as a result of the error.

Remember, even if the CRA is not bound by anything a CRA employee says or writes, and while listening to an employee may not be a good defence in court to support a taxpayer's incorrect actions, it is always important to document all dealings with the CRA. If a CRA employee has lead a taxpayer astray — either intentionally or accidentally through an error — the taxpayer can demonstrate that listening to the CRA caused his or her interest or penalties so he or she may successfully use this as a grounds for a request for taxpayer relief, and may be able to save thousands of dollars in interest and penalties.

While many taxpayers choose not to file a Notice of Objection and instead choose to file a Request for Taxpayer Relief (see Chapter 10), this strategy is ill-advised. I have heard of very few cases where taxpayers have been successful at obtaining relief without professional help. Taxpayers should realize that the relief process will still be available to them if they file a Notice of Objection and fail. However, the reverse is not always true due to the time constraints when filing an objection. Since it takes so many months for the CRA to review requests for relief, by the time a negative answer is received by the taxpayer, it is often too late to file an objection.

Documentation that may be required to substantiate a request for taxpayer relief on the grounds of the CRA having caused the problem includes maintaining a copy of all correspondence between the taxpayer and the CRA, as well as keeping a log of phone calls with

CRA employees, which include the subject of the conversation; notes about the conversation; the phone number called; the date and time of the conversation; and the name, ID number, and department of the employee spoken to. Without this information, there will be no way to prove that the conversation happened, and a relief request may be denied on that basis.

If the CRA is incorrect on an assessment, it will be important to make sure that documentation is available to rebut the assumptions. Without this documentation, there is likely no chance of success in challenging the assessment.

Once an objection has been filed and received by the CRA, it is not able to take collections action against a taxpayer in cases where the amounts in question are not trust debts (e.g., GST or HST, or payroll taxes). Even though the disputed amounts cannot be collected by the CRA, daily interest does accrue on the balance. When a taxpayer has been reassessed, regardless of whether he or she chooses to appeal the assessment, he or she should pay the amount in question. At least, if the objection fails, the taxpayer will not have the added burden of another year or more of interest. Believe it or not, some tax matters take years before an outcome is reached. Oftentimes there is no resolution until the matter has gone to court and, by then, if the matter is found against the taxpayer, with a whopping daily interest rate of prime plus 3 percent, interest may get to the point where the debt becomes unmanageable and the taxpayer may even have to declare bankruptcy.

Further, for those who are weary of paying a debt with which they disagree, it should be noted that the act of paying a tax bill as assessed is not an indication that the taxpayers agree with the assessment, and it does not prevent them from successfully challenging the

assessment. Paying when assessed is a smart fiscal decision which will avoid future interest. If a matter is found in favour of the taxpayers who have already paid, the CRA will issue a refund.

2.1 The objection process

You cannot appeal directly to the Tax Court of Canada. You also can't rely on your Member of Parliament (MP) or the Taxpayers' Ombudsman in order to resolve your incorrect assessment. Only in very exceptional circumstances will an MP be willing or able to assist, and the ombudsman is impotent when it comes to adjusting or reviewing a notice; the ombudsman's job is to help the taxpayer navigate the system with respect to service-level complaints about the CRA or its employees.

In order to initiate the objection process, you must complete a Notice of Objection (T400A) in writing and send it to the Chief of Appeals in a District Office or Taxation Centre (see subsection 165(2) of the act).

In the case of Lester v. The Queen (2004 TCC 179), the Tax Court of Canada ruled that an objection need not be sent on the T400A form in order to be valid (Lester sent an objection in the form of a letter); however, the objection must be in writing. My advice to the Canadian taxpayer is to file the objection on the form provided just in case the CRA chooses not to acknowledge some other form of objection. Plus, the form prompts the taxpayer to provide all necessary information from the date of the reassessment to the reasons for the objection.

In order to dispute a reassessment, a taxpayer must file a Notice of Objection. If the taxpayer files after the 90-day period permitted, he or she must also file with the objection an application for an extension, which is a written letter that requests the extension and provides the reasons for the request. While an assessment may generally be objected to within the 90-day period, and while the CRA is permitted to provide an extension and accept a late objection, it is best not to count on getting an extension. You're well advised to take your tax matters seriously and address all concerns within the time periods allowed. A great many of my clients have failed to do things within the correct time periods, which left them with very few options other than to have me hold off the CRA's dogs while they attempted to pay the unfair or incorrect debt over an extended period. Since some taxpayers missed their opportunity to object, the CRA's assessment became unchallengeable.

Once the CRA has received and processed the Notice of Objection, it sends a letter to the taxpayer and the taxpayer's representative acknowledging receipt of the objection. If the objection was received beyond the normal 90-day period without an application for an extension, the letter may reject the objection and advise a taxpayer to re-file the notice along with an application for extension. In other cases, where an application for an extension to file the objection accompanied the objection, the CRA can indicate in its letter its acceptance or denial of the extension request. If the request is denied, a taxpayer may apply to the Federal Court for Judicial Review of this decision. (See Chapter 14 for more information about fighting the CRA in court.)

Once an appeals officer is assigned by the Chief of Appeals, his or her job is to review the objection and the submissions of the taxpayer or his or her representative, along with working papers or reports from an audit and penalty reports, if available. There may be extensive communication between the appeals officer and the taxpayer, which can go on for weeks or months. In many cases I have seen appeals officers simply deny the taxpayer's objection and issue a Notice of Confirmation without having any contact with the taxpayer at all. I call this method the "stealth-file closing" because it is done without the knowledge of the taxpayer and his or her representative, denying the person the ability to fully make his or her case. This stealth-file closing is also particularly harmful as the taxpayer has no further recourse accept the Tax Court of Canada. If the taxpayer requires a lawyer, he or she can expect to pay thousands of dollars to convince the court of what he or she would likely have been able to convince the appeals officer had he or she been provided with an opportunity to do so.

If the appeals officer does not do a stealth-file closing of an objection, he or she will often ask the taxpayer to provide further documents, information, or other evidence to support the taxpayer's claims. Once all the requested backup materials have been provided and processed by the appeals officer, he or she generally indicates to the taxpayer which way he or she is going on the matter. Sometimes the auditor will provide the taxpayer with one last opportunity to convince the auditor of his or her point. After that, the appeals officer will prepare his or her Appeals Report (T401) which will outline his or her conclusions. Based on the conclusions, which are generally reviewed by the auditor's team leader, the appeals officer may reverse, vary, or confirm the assessment. Once this process is completed and a reassessment is issued, the next step in order to continue the objection process is to file an appeal with the Tax Court of Canada.

If you choose to object to a Notice of Assessment or Reassessment, you must decide whether to do it on your own or to hire a tax professional to assist you. While many taxpayers are successful on their own, before proceeding without help, you must be well informed about the law and the procedure, failing which you are at a serious disadvantage. Some accountants can help with an objection, but usually a tax lawyer is a better option. As opposed to an accountant, who may provide the correct accounting and numbers to the CRA, tax lawyers are trained to fight for your rights and to argue your position.

The following are some interesting statistics on objections:

- There are approximately 100,000 objections handled annually by the CRA's Appeals Branch.

- Less than 10 percent of taxpayers choose to go to the Tax Court of Canada following the objection process.

- Approximately one-third of all matters before the Tax Court of Canada are settled prior to trial. An equal number are withdrawn by the taxpayers prior to court.

3. Collections Action

One of the benefits of the objection process is that it can actually hold off collections action in certain cases. Even if a taxpayer may likely lose his or her objection, it can be strategic to file the Notice of Objection in order to hold off collections action.

For regular taxes (not including GST or HST, or payroll), once a Notice of Objection is filed and accepted by the CRA, the amounts being objected to are classified as "disputed amounts." For disputed amounts, the CRA is not able to pursue collections action. Instead it must wait for the amounts to be confirmed by the Appeals Officer, and if the confirmation is appealed to the Tax Court of Canada, the items continue to be uncollectible by the CRA until such time as the court has ruled on the case in favour of the CRA.

While the CRA is not able to take collections action to recover these disputed amounts, if any refunds or rebates are due to a taxpayer, the CRA is entitled by law to withhold these amounts and apply them to the unpaid balance. If the objection or court application is successful and amounts had been withheld by the CRA, it will be required to issue a refund cheque to the taxpayer for the amounts in question.

Unlike objections to income tax assessments, objections that relate to GST or HST or source deductions (i.e., payroll) amounts, do not prevent the CRA from taking collections action. The difference stems from the fact that GST or HST and payroll amounts are considered to be "trust" monies that are collected for and held in trust on behalf of the CRA, and when taxpayers collect or withhold these amounts, the CRA wants to collect them. As far as the CRA is concerned, these amounts should be held separate from the taxpayer's regular funds, and should be available for payment to the CRA. Since these amounts are trust amounts, the CRA has no restrictions in terms of collections action — even while the amounts are being disputed within the CRA or within the Tax Court of Canada.

Even though the CRA is not able to collect the disputed amounts, if they are left unpaid, they are subject to ongoing daily interest — even while the objection process or court proceeding is ongoing. As such, if a taxpayer can pay the amount in question, whether or not he or she believes the objection will be successful, the person is advised to do so.

The advantage to paying as soon as possible is clear. If the objection is unsuccessful, the taxpayer will save a bundle in interest charges by paying immediately. If the taxpayer is successful, the CRA will issue a refund for any overpayment with interest. Further, despite the fact that some taxpayers believe that paying is akin to agreeing to the CRA's numbers, whether or not a taxpayer has paid his or her taxes will not affect the outcome of his or her objection or court application.

4. Penalties

In 2009 and 2010, the CRA audited approximately 380,000 small- and medium-sized businesses and issued Notices of Reassessment requiring these businesses to pay $2.1 billion in tax, interest, and penalties, and there is no doubt that interest and penalties accounted for several hundred million dollars over those two years. Besides being applied in the case of audits, penalties are routinely applied by the CRA for a number of reasons, most commonly, for late filing and inaccurate returns.

Even more serious than the application of penalties is the possibility of being prosecuted by the CRA for failing to comply with requirements to deduct, remit, or report, a taxpayer may be prosecuted. Fines range from $1,000 to $25,000 and prison terms of up to 12 months may apply for each offence.

4.1 Late filing penalties of income tax returns

Probably the most common penalty applied by the CRA is late filing of an income tax return, which is 5 percent of the unpaid taxes plus an additional 1 percent for each month the return is late, up to a maximum of 12 months. The maximum penalty is 17 percent if the return is filed over a year late.

For repeat offenders, the CRA has an increased penalty. In cases where taxpayers have already been assessed late filing penalties for one or more of the previous three years, the taxpayer may be subject to the repeat offender penalty, which is equal to 10 percent of the unpaid taxes plus an additional 2 percent per month for a period of up to 20 months — or a maximum of 50 percent if the return is filed more than 20 months late. Since the CRA steps up their penalties for repeat offenders, oftentimes late filers are best advised to file all of their outstanding returns at once. Those who file a few returns at a time in order to catch up may find that they have been assessed the regular late filing penalty on the first batch of returns filed late, and the second batch, even if filed shortly thereafter, may trigger the repeat offender penalty.

In Quebec, taxpayers are required to file both a provincial and a federal return since Quebec, unlike other provinces, administers its own provincial tax rather than allowing the CRA to do so on its behalf. In Quebec, the rules are often similar, and late filing penalties are one such area. As with the rest of the country, in Quebec, if taxpayers file late, they are charged a 5 percent penalty on balances not paid by the filing deadline. If the taxpayers pay the full amount by the filing deadline, yet file their returns late, the 5 percent penalty is not invoked, and instead the taxpayers will be subject to a 1 percent penalty for every complete month their return is late, with a 12-month maximum. Taxpayers who file late and have not paid in full will incur both the penalty of 5 percent of the unpaid balance and 1 percent for every late month. So, if the taxpayers have not paid anything and file 12 months late, they will be subject to a maximum penalty of 17 percent.

4.2 Late filing of GST or HST

Late filing penalties also apply to GST, HST, source deductions, and Quebec Sales Tax. These penalties are quite different in Quebec from the rest of the country. In Quebec, the penalties for late filing of source deductions and sales tax are assessed at a penalty of 7 percent if the filing is late by 7 days or less, 11 percent if the filing is more than 7 days and less than 15 days late, and 15 percent when the filing is late by 15 or more days.

The CRA has a simpler and less costly penalty structure for GST and HST returns. For GST and HST, the penalty for late filing is calculated by the formula A + (B x C). A is 1 percent of the amount owing; B is 25 percent of A, and C is the number of months overdue to a maximum of 12. For example, if a taxpayer who is late in filing his or her GST or HST return by 12 months, and owes $10,000, the CRA's formula looks like this:

- $100 + (25 x 12) = $400, which comes out to a 4 percent penalty. In Quebec, since the filing would have been more than 14 days late, this penalty would have been 15 percent or $1,500.

For source deductions, the CRA assesses penalties for late remittances (payments) of 3 percent if the amount is one to three days late, 5 percent if it is four to five days late, 7 percent if it is six to seven days late, and 10 percent if it is more than seven days late or if no amount was remitted. Further, in cases where the taxpayer has been subject to the penalty once already in a particular calendar year, all subsequent failures may be assessed a penalty of 20 percent if such failures were made knowingly or under circumstances of gross negligence. For instance, if a taxpayer owes $10,000 and is 30 days late, he or she would be subject to a penalty of 10 percent or $1,000, which would increase to $2,000 on a subsequent failure. In Quebec, a penalty of 15 percent or $1,500 would apply.

For further information on penalty amounts for GST and HST returns when the CRA has issued a demand to file, and where a taxpayer was required to file electronically but did not, or where the taxpayer failed to accurately report information, please refer to the CRA's web page entitled "Penalties and Interest" in the business section. (At the time of printing, the following link takes you to the information: www.cra-arc.gc.ca/tx/bsnss/tpcs/gst-tps/bspsbch/rtrns/pnlts-eng.html.)

4.3 Repeat failure to report income penalty

Different from the late filing penalty, the penalty for repeat failure to report income consists of both a federal portion and a provincial portion, except for Quebec, where the CRA only deals with federal taxes in that province. In order for this penalty to be applied, the taxpayer must have failed to report an amount of income on one of the three previous years, and must have been reassessed for that year. For example, in order for the penalty to apply to the 2012 assessment, the taxpayer must have failed to report income in 2009, 2010, or 2011, and was subsequently reassessed by the CRA for one or more of these years.

The amount of this penalty is substantial, and is applied in the amount of 20 percent (i.e., 10 percent for the federal portion and 10 percent for the provincial portion). In Quebec, the CRA simply applies a 10 percent penalty.

4.4 Gross negligence penalties

The most severe penalty which can be assessed by the CRA is the gross negligence penalty which is assessed under subsection 163(2) of the act when the taxpayer "knowingly or under circumstances amounting to gross negligence, has made or has participated in, assented to or acquiesced in the making of, a false statement or an omission in a return."

This type of penalty of 50 percent of the tax owing is designed to ensure that taxpayers complete their returns correctly and honestly, and since this particular penalty is so severe, the burden of proof is actually shifted to the CRA; that is, the CRA bears the burden of proving that the penalty was justified and appropriately applied.

These penalties are often applied by auditors when they are not justified, and in any case, a taxpayer is best served by challenging these penalties. I have seen many cases in which taxpayers have been scammed by slick-confidence men, and as a result of the scam, they have filed their tax returns incorrectly. (See Chapter 15 for more information about tax schemes.) In these cases, not only did these taxpayers lose money to the scammers, but they also had the gross negligence penalty unfairly applied.

According to Canadian courts, the gross negligence penalty is not to be applied lightly. Since subsection 163(2) of the act is penal, it is not sufficient that on the balance of probabilities (50 percent or greater) the CRA believes the taxpayer is deserving of the penalty. Much more is required. So, if the taxpayer can introduce any doubt as to whether these penalties are warranted, he or she may be able to avoid having the penalties applied.

In cases where the CRA has not yet audited or reassessed a taxpayer, if he or she believes that an error or omission may justify a reassessment and the application of gross negligence penalties, and if the person meets the requirements for the program (see Chapter 10 for information about interest and penalty relief), taxpayers are strongly advised to consider filing a Voluntary Disclosure. If successful, the Voluntary Disclosure Program (VDP) provides for an amnesty for prosecution and penalties. Interest rates are reduced in these cases. Taxpayers should seek legal counsel if they are considering applying under the program.

4.5 Penalty for late or insufficient installment payments

In cases where taxpayers are required to remit installment payments to the CRA, they can be charged penalties when their payments are late or less than the required amount. The penalty is applicable only if installment interest is greater than $1,000, and is determined by the following:

- The CRA determines which amount is greater: $1,000 or 25 percent of the interest that would apply in the year had installment payments not been made.

- The CRA takes this number and subtracts it from the actual installment interest charged in the year, and divides the number by 2. For example, if an individual made late installment payments in a year and was charged $4,000 of interest, and had he or she not paid any installments, the person would have be charged $6,000 of interest, since 25 percent of $6,000 ($1,500) is greater than $1,000, subtract $1,500 from $4,000 and then divide by 2, which gives a penalty of $1,250.

4.6 Third-party civil penalties

There are a great number of ways that a return can be fraudulently manipulated in order to claim inflated personal or business expenses, false deductions, credits, or exemptions. Sometimes these manipulations are made by the taxpayer in an attempt to reduce his or her taxes, and other times they are performed by the individual preparing the taxpayer's return — frequently without the taxpayer's consent or knowledge.

While most tax return preparers are honest, you should carefully read through your return and not sign it until such time as you are confident that its contents are true and accurate.

In most cases, when the CRA discovers a fraudulent tax return, it will impose penalties (and possible criminal charges) on the taxpayer, who will also be charged daily interest on those amounts. Even in cases where the taxpayer was tricked or conned into filing an incorrect return, the CRA takes little pity and will still apply these penalties. This is notwithstanding the fact that the CRA has a set of penalties designed especially for third parties who commit fraud on the taxpayer's behalf, or cause the taxpayer to commit the fraud.

These third-party civil penalties are divided into two broad categories: planner penalties and preparer penalties. In order to apply either one of these two third-party civil penalties, the CRA must establish that the individual made a false statement. (For further information on the Third-Party Civil Penalties, please consult the CRA's Information Circular IC01-1, available on the CRA website.)

4.6a Planner penalty

The planner penalty, according to the CRA, need not be identified in order for the penalty to apply, but is defined as "a person who makes, furnishes, participates in the making of, or causes another person to make or furnish a statement that the person knows, or would reasonably be expected to know but for circumstances amounting to culpable conduct, is a false statement that could be used by another person for a purpose of the ITA [*Income Tax Act*] or for a purpose of the ETA [*Excise Tax Act*]." Such people could include tax-shelter promoters and people involved in the planning of tax schemes.

The planner penalty can be up to the greater of $1,000 or of the total of the person's gross entitlements for the planning activity.

4.6b Preparer penalty

The preparer penalty, despite its name, is not limited to those individuals who actually prepare tax returns. It can apply to individuals who are also "planners." The CRA describes a preparer as "a person who makes, or participates in, assents to, or acquiesces in the making of a statement to, by or on behalf of another person that the person knows, or would reasonably be expected to know but for circumstances amounting to culpable conduct, is a false statement that could be used by or on behalf of the other person for a purpose of the ITA or ETA." Those who could have the preparer penalty applied against them include tax return preparers, tax advisors, and others.

Penalties for preparers can be as high as the sum of $100,000 and the person's gross compensation earned for the false statement.

5. Interest

I would rather owe money to a loan shark than owe money to the CRA. On the one hand, the loan shark does not have the power to seize my house and my assets or close down my company. On the other hand, the loan shark would likely offer me a better interest rate, which would not accrue daily!

The interest rate charged by the CRA can fluctuate each quarter, and the CRA applies interest charges on all amounts that are past due. Further, when the CRA applies late penalties, interest is charged on those penalty amounts from the day the filing was due. If penalties are applied for older years in the course of reassessments following the audits, retroactive interest can be applied from the year to which the penalty applied.

10
INTEREST AND PENALTY RELIEF

Due to the fact that many taxpayers are crippled by tax debts which include large amounts of interest and penalties, Parliament has decided to include provisions in the Canadian tax laws which allow for the reduction of interest and penalties in certain circumstances.

One way to reduce interest and penalties is through the Taxpayer Relief Program, and the other way is through the Voluntary Disclosures Program (VDP), which is designed to encourage taxpayers to come forward and voluntarily disclose income which had previously not been declared to the Canada Revenue Agency (CRA).

1. Taxpayer Relief Program

The Taxpayer Relief program, formerly known as "Fairness," empowers the CRA by law to waive interest and penalties at its discretion. Perhaps because the system is not always fair,

or because the CRA did not want to be thought of as being fair, this program was renamed.

Taxpayers must remember that the principal tax amount cannot be altered through this program, and it is only interest and penalty amounts which can be forgiven. If a taxpayer is burdened with a debt to the CRA, which includes interest and/or penalties, in order to potentially receive a reduction of interest and penalties, the taxpayer can complete the Request for Taxpayer Relief (RC4288).

Item 12 in the Taxpayer Bill of Rights indicates that under legislation a taxpayer has the "right to interest and penalty relief because of extraordinary circumstances," and despite this legislated right, if taxpayers simply complete the three-page form on their own, unless they have a bulletproof case, I would not expect any sort of fairness. I believe that self-prepared requests for taxpayer relief fail in the majority of cases. When I talk about a bulletproof case, I usually offer this story to my clients:

Imagine a person who always filed his taxes on time, yet one year he became injured in an automobile accident. He fell into a coma and was kept on life-support for five years, and then woke up one day and was fine. Shortly after he woke up, he had his tax returns prepared, and filed them late. While a late-filing penalty would automatically apply to these late-filed returns, I am sure that the taxpayer relief committee would grant relief to such a person who could prove that he was physically unable to file the returns when due as a result of a medical situation. It would be unfair not to.

However, if a taxpayer's case is not bulletproof, and the person has not been on life-support for the better part of a decade, the person has to ensure that he or she qualifies for the program by meeting the relevant criteria, and he or she has prepared a case that is as strong as possible. This person also has to know why some applications have succeeded and others have failed. The taxpayer needs to know all the various reasons that the CRA typically uses to reject an application, from a lack of evidence, to the taxpayer having a poor compliance history, to the taxpayer not providing sufficient details. The taxpayer should also understand that if he or she is granted relief, it often only relates to certain years and is usually only partial relief.

Sometimes, if a taxpayer requires an extended period of time in order to pay the debt, he or she can receive relief of part or all of the interest going forward while the debt is being repaid as long as promised payments are made on time.

A taxpayer can qualify for interest and penalty relief in three basic ways:

1. **Extraordinary circumstances:** If the interest and/or penalties arose as a result of circumstances beyond the reasonable control of the taxpayer (e.g., accidents, severe illnesses, mental distress, fires, floods, or other disasters).

2. **Financial:** If a debt to the CRA, with its interest and penalties, is causing financial hardship, or if a taxpayer has demonstrated inability to pay the debt.

3. **Actions of the CRA:** If actions of the CRA, such as processing delays or errors, have caused or contributed to the interest and penalties.

Before taxpayers can file a request for taxpayer relief, they must ensure that they have filed all their returns to date. The CRA will not provide relief to delinquent taxpayers. In order to be granted relief, taxpayers must have a payment plan in place with the CRA.

To learn more about Interest and Penalty Relief, please consult the CRA's Information Circular IC07-1, "Taxpayer Relief Provisions."

Sometimes it is not enough that you have been in a coma for five years and unable to file. Sometimes the CRA will look at your past history before considering a grant for relief. A number of factors are considered by the CRA when it decides whether or not to grant relief. These factors do not come from legislation, but come from the CRA itself.

Remember, the CRA does not write the law — it only administers it. So, when the CRA uses a list of factors that it has created in order to prevent a taxpayer from gaining relief under a law written by parliament it may not be applying the law as it was intended. In such cases, it is possible for the taxpayer to have the matter examined by a judge of the Federal Court in order to judicially review whether the CRA's denial of the taxpayer's application based on such a factor was reasonable. Such factors include a taxpayer's compliance history, whether the taxpayer knowingly allowed a balance to exist, and whether the taxpayer has been negligent or careless in his or her filings.

1.1 Extraordinary circumstances

There are many circumstances beyond a taxpayer's control which could lead to the application of interest and penalties. For example, if the taxpayer is a victim of a man-made disaster such as a fire which destroyed an office and all records, or a natural disaster such as a storm flooding the taxpayer's house and washing away all the ink on all receipts. When such circumstances have occurred, the Taxpayer Bill of Rights says that a taxpayer has the "right to relief from penalties and interest under tax legislation because of extraordinary circumstances."

Besides the case of natural and man-made disasters, the CRA may also waive or decrease interest and penalties in cases where the taxpayer has been the victim of crime, has suffered from a substance abuse problem, has been depressed, or has a gambling addiction. In addition, the CRA will consider cancelling penalties and interest when a taxpayer has suffered a serious illness or accident or when the taxpayer is under serious emotional or mental distress.

However, don't expect the CRA to offer relief to a taxpayer simply because he or she has a sob story. The CRA usually requires that the sob story coincide with the taxpayer's failure to file or pay when required. For example, if the person was to use the hospitalization for a terrible accident as the grounds for relief, if he or she was in hospital from March to December 2012, and missed the 2011 filing, the person could likely expect to be able to get relief from the late filing penalties for the 2011 tax year. The CRA may even grant interest relief for all

debts during the time of the hospitalization if the taxpayer was not able to make his or her payments during that period. However, if the next few years were also filed late for no good reason, the taxpayer would likely not receive relief for any of those years.

1.2 Financial grounds

I speak to taxpayers every day who have debts to the CRA which are so high that they cannot even afford to pay the interest charges, even though they keep paying what they can every month, their debts keep on growing. It would appear for these taxpayers, as though they could never pay off the debt without selling everything they own. Many choose bankruptcy as an alternative (see Chapter 12 for more information about bankruptcy). The good news is that in many cases, when they consider the true amount of tax principal without the interest and penalties, with the same monthly payment, these taxpayers would be able to pay down their tax debts within a few short years. The bad news is that most taxpayers do not know about the taxpayer relief program, and many others have not adequately made the case to the CRA that they are deserving of relief. The key is to demonstrate to the CRA that with the reduction of interest and penalties they would be able to retire the debt in a reasonable time frame, and that without, financial ruin is a real possibility.

If a taxpayer can demonstrate that payment of the debt with interest and penalties would result in his or her inability to meet his or her basic necessities of life such as shelter, food, medical needs, heat, and transportation, he or she may receive relief on the grounds of financial hardship. Furthermore, if the taxpayer can demonstrate that he or she is unable to pay the debt within a reasonable time frame, or where he or she cannot service the debt with accruing interest, he or she too may receive relief under the grounds of a confirmed inability to pay.

What is important is that in order to receive relief, you must document your case. You must provide financial records and details including your assets and liabilities as well as income and monthly expenses. The CRA can and will scrutinize every expense, and if it discovers you're driving a $3,500 per month Bentley, it will not give you relief. If the CRA discovers that you have a summer cottage, you will not receive relief. Your expenses must be reasonable, and you must have done everything you can in order to pay off the debt before the CRA grants relief. It wants to see that you have applied (and been rejected) for loans. The CRA wants to see that you have sold your summer cottage and that you have sold, leased, and hypothecated everything down to your undergarments before granting relief for financial grounds.

1.3 Actions by the CRA

Sometimes an error or failure on the part of the CRA is the cause of a taxpayer's interest and penalties, and when this is the case, a taxpayer may make a case for relief. When it can be shown that the CRA was the cause, or even part of the cause, it should be documented on the request for taxpayer relief form.

In Information Circular IC07-1, the CRA cites six different types of occasions where taxpayers' interest and penalties may be waived. These are when the interest or penalties were as a result of —

- processing delays that result in the taxpayer not being informed of his or her debt within a reasonable time,

- errors in CRA publications,

- incorrect information provided to a taxpayer by the CRA,

- processing errors,

- delays in providing information to a taxpayer, or

- undue delays in completing an audit or resolving an objection or appeal.

1.4 Ten-year limitation

Because of the Federal Court of Appeal decision in Bozzer v. Canada, the CRA's discretion now allows for the cancellation or waiver of interest that accrued during the ten calendar years preceding the calendar year in which the request for relief is made, regardless of the year in which the tax debt arose.

Before the Bozzer case, taxpayers could not get any relief of interest that had accrued on a debt for a tax year that is, for example, 12 years old, even though it may be the interest from the last few years that is crushing the taxpayer. Nowadays, the last 10 years of interest may be cancelled under the program even on the 12-year old debt.

2. Voluntary Disclosures Program (VDP)

Sometimes called amnesty, the other occasion on which penalties and interest may be relieved is when taxpayers have filed an application under the Voluntary Disclosures Program (VDP).

Designed to encourage Canadian taxpayers to declare previously undeclared income, and fix previously overstated expenses, the CRA rewards those who qualify, with acceptance, which means that they will not be prosecuted, penalties will not apply, and interest is usually decreased. What this means is that if the taxpayers qualify, they can save themselves a bundle in interest and penalties.

The only catch is this is one area where I would strongly suggest that a taxpayer get assistance from a tax lawyer. The problem with a person doing a voluntary disclosure without a lawyer's assistance is that the taxpayer can get into a lot of trouble if the disclosure fails. During the course of voluntary disclosure, a taxpayer is required to provide a complete and accurate disclosure of his or her income and expenses. This means that without the proper intermediary between the taxpayer and the CRA, in the case of a failed disclosure, the CRA has been provided with all the information it needs to possibly prosecute a taxpayer for tax evasion.

When a taxpayer uses a lawyer, the process is generally commenced anonymously, and if he or she gets cold feet, the person can decide to back out of the program before the process is completed. In cases where a taxpayer applies on his or her own or by using an accountant, the person doesn't have the option of backing out. In those cases, the CRA either knows the identity of the taxpayer if the taxpayer applied on his or her own, or the CRA can require that the accountant who filed the disclosure divulge the identity of the taxpayer as well as any other piece of information that the CRA requires.

In order to qualify for a voluntary disclosure, a taxpayer must meet four conditions:

- The amount in question must be subject to a penalty.

- The information must be at least one year overdue.

- The disclosure must be complete.

- The disclosure must be voluntary — once a taxpayer has been asked to file returns or is being investigated for the time period in question, his or her cooperation ceases to be voluntary and becomes coerced.

3. Administrative Appeals

If a request for taxpayer relief is not granted by the CRA, a taxpayer cannot mount a challenge by filing a Notice of Objection or an appeal to the Tax Court of Canada. Instead, the taxpayer is required to file for a second review of the taxpayer relief application, and if still unsuccessful, an application to Federal Court for judicial review of the decision of the CRA. Since taxpayer relief is an area in which the CRA is empowered to exercise its discretion, the exercise of this discretion can be reviewed by the Federal Court in a process called "judicial review."

While the Federal Court will review whether the CRA properly exercised its discretion, it will not normally substitute its judgment for that of the CRA. Typically the court will simply order that the CRA re-review the application, which in my guess, more often than not, results in the granting of the application. If a taxpayer chooses to apply for judicial review, he or she must do so within 30 days of the time the CRA issues its decision.

Before going to court because relief was denied, the taxpayer must first request a second-level review of the application. At this point, the taxpayer may include any other relevant materials which would help the CRA in reaching a decision in his or her favour. This second review of the application is performed by a CRA official who was not involved in the decision on the initial application. Only if the taxpayer is dissatisfied with the decision of this second review may he or she apply to have the matter heard in Federal Court.

SAMPLE 2
REQUEST FOR TAXPAYER RELIEF

<table>
<tr><td>🍁 Canada Revenue
Agency</td><td>Agence du revenu
du Canada</td></tr>
</table>

REQUEST FOR TAXPAYER RELIEF

Please read the "Information to assist in completing this form" on the last page before completing this form.

Section I – IDENTIFICATION

Taxpayer name	Account number(s) for this request
John Doe	**Individual: Social insurance number** 123 456 789

Mailing address	Employer:
123 Street	_____ RP ___
	GST/HST Registrant: _____ RT ___
	Corporation: _____ RC ___

City	Prov./Terr./State	Other: account number, type of return etc.
Toronto	ON	

Postal code/Zip code	Country (if other than Canada)
M5V 2T2	

Telephone: Home   4 1 6 - 5 5 5 - 5 5 5 5   Work   ___ - ___ - ___

Section 2 – DETAILS OF REQUEST

1. Type of request:

   a) ☐ Penalty: cancellation or waiver: *Specify type of penalty and amount, if known* _____

   b) ☐ Interest: cancellation or waiver: *Specify type of interest and amount, if known* _____

   c) ☐ Refund or reduction in amounts payable beyond the normal three year period (individual and testamentary trust accounts)

   d) ☐ Late, amended or revoked election: *Specify type of election* _____

2. Reason(s):

   Indicate the reason(s) for your request under the taxpayer relief provisions. Please note no reason is necessary when asking for a refund or reduction in amounts payable beyond the normal three year period.

   ☐ Canada Revenue Agency error   ☐ Natural or man-made disaster

   ☐ Canada Revenue Agency delay   ☐ Death/accident/serious illness/emotional or mental distress

   ☐ Financial hardship/inability to pay   ☐ Civil disturbance

   ☐ Other extraordinary circumstances: *Specify* _____

   _____

RC4288 E (11)   (Vous pouvez obtenir ce formulaire en français à **www.arc.gc.ca** ou au **1-800-959-3376**)   Canada

3. Year/periods involved

For individuals/corporations: indicate the taxation years/taxation year-ends _____

For employers: indicate the pay periods or type of information return involved _____

For GST registrants: indicate the reporting periods involved _____

For other: indicate period(s)/years(s) involved _____

4. Second review:

Is this a request for a second review?   No ☐   Answer only question 5 below

                                              Yes ☐   Answer only question 6 below

5. Information needed to support your request:
This question does not apply for requests for refunds or reduction in amounts payable beyond the normal three year period.

Describe all the circumstances and facts supporting your taxpayer relief request. Please include a history of events including, if applicable, any measures that you have taken to correct/avoid this tax situation. You may enclose a letter with this form to provide the information.

_____
_____
_____
_____
_____
_____
_____
_____
_____
_____
_____
_____
_____
_____
_____
_____
_____
_____
_____
_____

6. Reasons to support a second review:

State the reasons why you disagree with the decision made in regards to the first review. You may enclose a letter with this form to provide the information. Please include any new documentation to support this request for a second review.

_____
_____
_____
_____
_____
_____
_____
_____
_____
_____
_____
_____
_____
_____
_____
_____
_____
_____

Section 3 – SUPPORTING DOCUMENTATION

Please submit all relevant documentation to support your request. See examples of supporting documentation in the attached "Information to assist in completing this form".

Section 4 – CERTIFICATION

If you are a representative, please provide your name and phone number and, if not already submitted to the Canada Revenue Agency, an authorization form (T1013 for individual/trust accounts or a RC59 for business accounts).

_____
Name of representative

Title

_____
Signature of taxpayer or representative

Phone number: 416-555-5555

Year	Month	Day
2012	06	11

Date

4. Remission Orders

If a taxpayer is in the unfortunate position where it is either too late to pursue traditional remedies such as objections, administrative reviews, and appeals to the court, or where all the other remedies have failed, he or she has one last-ditch attempt to obtain relief, and this involves having the federal government grant a remission order to cancel his or her tax owing. A remission order may be granted in extreme cases where it would be seriously unfair to make somebody pay his or her amount owing which could not be cancelled or reduced other than by a remission order.

Since a remission order has to be approved by many levels of the CRA before even reaching the government, the process can take years, and taxpayers should not count on receiving one. Only a few are granted each year and they are for particularly exceptional cases.

11
CRA COLLECTIONS

The Canada Revenue Agency (CRA) employs approximately 300 full-time collections officers who are generally assigned by the CRA to collect a debt that is larger than $20,000. Taxpayers that have been flagged in the past may be followed by a collections officer for a few years, pursuing smaller amounts.

If you are self-employed, or run a small business, CRA collections officers can become an important and stressful part of your daily life, and they can have very dramatic effects on the operation of your business, your relationships with your clients, your ability to receive your income, and the quality of your personal life.

Many people live their entire lives without speaking with a CRA collections officer. If you work for somebody else, and he or she deducts your taxes at source from your paycheque, you may never hear from a collections officer. Un-

less you are self-employed; have large investments; or are involved in a transaction that results in a capital gain on real estate, stocks, precious metals, or you make a large withdrawal from an RRSP, you will likely deal with an agent in the CRA's general call centre in regards to your tax debts.

1. Collection Call from the Call Centre

Many taxpayers first get a call from the CRA's call centre asking them to make payment on a debt. These calls are generally made approximately 45 days after an assessment has been issued, which are sometimes referred to as "collection call #7."

Call centre agents collect small amounts owing and act as a first line of contact after an assessment is issued. Call centre agents can request payment of a debt regardless of the amount, but they do not exercise collection powers to enforce the debt. Call centre agents will tell you that their guidelines require full payment within 30 days; however, they will generally agree to any arrangement up to 6 months and have the ability to extend payment up to 12 months if they collect 25 percent of the debt up-front in the first payment. Arrangements made by the call centre can be overridden by a collections officer. In other words, if you make a deal with the call centre, a future collections officer is not obligated to respect it and may subject you to a second round of negotiation and collection enforcement.

2. The Collections Officer

Collections officers are employees of the CRA empowered to collect tax debts under the *Income Tax Act* and the *Excise Tax Act*. They have very broad powers to collect the debt owed to the CRA, and these collections officers differ from private collection agency employees in five important ways:

- They have the ability to request information about you from your financial institutions, your clients, and your suppliers.

- They have the ability to enforce debts via the confiscation of funds from bank accounts, the garnishment of funds from paycheques, and the interception of funds in commercial transactions.

- They have the ability to place liens against real estate, vehicles, and other assets. They have the ability to recommend that the Department of Justice seize these assets and sell them at a sheriff's auction.

- They do not have the discretion to waive interest or settle a debt at a partial amount. They only have discretion on how long they will wait for payment to be made.

- Their primary objective is to close the file as quickly as possible. They do not necessarily care if their collection actions break a business and make collection of the debt impossible. They do not receive a commission on the amounts they collect. They are incentivized purely in terms of the statistics related to how quickly they close a file and how many files they close.

Many entrepreneurs find that years of experience in dealing with creditors and collection disputes are of no help in dealing with a CRA collections officer. The entrepreneur simply does not understand the culture and motivations of the collections officer. They live in different worlds. While the entrepreneur is accustomed to feast and famine in terms of revenue volatility, the collector lives in a predictable world where government paycheques arrive, like clockwork, every two weeks. While the entrepreneur sees everything as working capital to keep a business alive, a collections officer sees the payment of taxes as a sacred trust. The entrepreneur sees himself or herself as a noble creator of economic activity and employment. The collections officer sees the entrepreneur as a loose cannon and a free agent with questionable ethics. While the entrepreneur sees the collector as a civil servant, an economic parasite, the collections officer wakes up every day believing that he or she is the good guy going after the bad guys.

Collections officers consider themselves professionals. The CRA is similar to a department store in the sense that its employees often work in various departments throughout their career. Although there are certain specializations such as audits that require specific credentials (e.g., an accounting licence), most of the positions in the CRA are learned via in-house apprenticeship.

The typical CRA employee has a moderate education, with possibly a community college certificate. He or she tends to join the CRA at a young age, often becoming aware of openings via friends and relatives already employed by the agency. If you are speaking with a 30-year-old CRA employee, that person often has eight to ten years of job experience and may have worked in non-filer, enforcement, voluntary disclosures, and other departments before doing collections. As such, the person may consider himself or herself an expert on the entire tax system. This, combined with his or her considerable discretionary powers, empowers a collections officer with confidence and power. He or she may view his or her job as the arm of a sovereign state, and is impatient with those who impede his or her objectives.

Taxpayers may, over the course of several years, accumulate a series of broken promises, new debts, and other compliance failures, such as unfiled returns. Taxpayers in such a position, especially those who are self-employed or owners of a business, will often end up on the list of a "closer." A closer is a collections officer who specializes in closing bad tax accounts. These closer collections officers are typically more senior, and have been given wide discretion by their superiors to be especially aggressive in order to bring a file to a close in a short period of time. Closers do not especially care if they recover the debt owing to the government. They are more interested in stopping what they see as a pattern of a self-employed person or business from accumulating any further debt, and wasting the time of the CRA.

If a taxpayer has a history of broken promises (a "bad diary" in CRA parlance), or if a collections supervisor feels that a business has been counting on its GST or payroll trust monies as cash flow to survive on an ongoing basis, a senior collections officer may attempt to "shut down" the sole proprietorship or business. This will never be recorded as an official decision, but the effect will be that of total destruction of a business. A combination of bank account seizures, letters to clients advising them to remit their payments to the CRA instead, and seizure of equipment essential to operate a business may all occur within a short period of time. Offers by the taxpayer to make interim payments to negotiate the situation will be ignored or rejected. In such cases, the taxpayer's representative can sometimes save the business, but only by offering substantial balloon payments up-front, which for many entrepreneurs in that position is simply impossible.

The goal of a collections officer is to collect a debt as quickly as possible, or if that is not possible, to apply maximum pressure to bring a taxpayer into compliance with a repayment plan. The collections officer will often look for cash or its equivalents in terms of real estate equity which can be hypothecated with a second mortgage or line of credit, or the liquidation of assets such as stocks or RRSPs. The CRA may be patient in terms of liquidating an asset such as RRSP monies if withdrawals cause additional destruction of wealth due to marginal rates at withdrawal time. A collections officer will cooperate with a taxpayer if he or she feels that the taxpayer is communicating with him or her in good faith and providing the information needed in order to assess the taxpayer's ability to repay a debt. For any negotiation involving a significant tax debt, the collections officer will request the following:

- **Income and expense, net worth worksheets:** These worksheets show the cash in and out that supports a person or enterprise, as well as the assets and liabilities that comprise his or her net worth.

- **Participation by the spouse in both disclosure and repayment:** The CRA has stopped trying to hold spouses formally accountable for the actions of their partners. However, the CRA expects that the household's ability to repay be taken into account when an interim payment plan is negotiated. This means full disclosure of income and expense and net worth by the partner of a taxpayer with a tax debt, as well as participation in the repayment of the debt either via cash payments or assumption of household expenses in order to liberate cash flow to be allocated to the debt. Otherwise, the collections officer may simply refuse to negotiate an interim payment plan and may proceed to more aggressive collections measures.

- **Bank statements, invoices, client lists, and receivables list for the last three to six months:** Taxpayers are often reluctant to provide the names of their clients to CRA collections officers. Their fear, which is not without justification, is that the collections officers will simply turn around and attempt to intercept the trade receivables (i.e., accounts receivable amounts that are due to a business or a self-employed individual by their clients). The reality of the situation is somewhat different. Collections officers try to intercept a trade receivable if they feel that there is no other way to satisfy a debt. However, refusing to provide this information will usually irritate the collections officers and make the situation worse. In general, if a collections officer asks a self-employed person or business for the names of the clients, the taxpayer should do so by faxing a letter in which he or she provides the information along with the following sentences: "I am providing this information in good

faith. I expect the CRA to continue to deal with me in good faith and refrain from garnishing this receivable while we negotiate an interim payment plan."

- **Attempts to obtain financing:** This is especially important. A collections officer will say something to the effect that "we aren't your bank," and insist that a taxpayer approach his or her bank for a loan or line of credit with which to repay all or part of the debt. A letter from a bank refusing financing is usually sufficient to address this query. If a taxpayer does refinance his or her home, the person should ensure that he or she takes the increased monthly mortgage payment into account when promising additional monthly payments against a tax debt.

3. National Collections Centres

In addition to collecting debts owed by individuals and corporations for income tax, the CRA runs national collections centres that collect smaller GST, Employment Insurance (EI), Canada Pension Plan (CPP), and payroll debts, as well as some T2 (corporate) tax debts. These collection centres typically work outbound in that the employees call the taxpayers.

The collection centres differ from the general call centre in that they exercise collection powers. For example, if you have a GST debt owing, you may get a call from a collector based in Winnipeg, Saskatoon, or Bathurst. They have the power to seize your bank account, and often do so as their first form of contact. In other words, if you ignore a letter asking you to pay a GST debt, there is a strong chance that your company or individual bank account will be frozen and emptied without a phone call from a CRA agent.

4. When the Debt Becomes Collectable

A debt to the CRA becomes collectable 90 days after the date of a Notice of Assessment or Reassessment. This is primarily a convention — the CRA does not typically initiate collections action during this time in order to give you time to file an objection, should you wish to do so.

After an assessment is issued, the CRA will follow up with a generic letter and a phone call from the call centre. If the debt is large, or concerns a trust amount, a collections officer will be assigned immediately, and will send a letter after 10 days, and a phone call after 45 days. Collections officers may also be assigned to collect relatively small amounts if a taxpayer has a history of late payments or late filing of returns.

A taxpayer may receive a number of notices over the course of a quiet year, a voice mail or two from the call centre, then suddenly get a menacing call from a collector demanding immediate payment of the debt, with the threat of legal action including bank account, payroll, and trade receivable seizure if he or she fails to comply. Ignoring letters and voicemail messages from collections officers only irritates the officers and results in less flexibility and harsher treatment of a file.

5. Trust Debts versus Income Tax Debts

The CRA views certain taxes as being "trust debts" or "trust amounts." These are amounts which have been collected by the taxpayer or withheld by the taxpayer on behalf of the government and include GST or HST, payroll taxes, EI, and CPP.

The CRA views the collection of a trust debt as being a very serious matter. In the CRA's view, a taxpayer has been deputized as the collector for the taxes; in other words, the money never belonged to the taxpayer in the first place and should not have been used by the taxpayer for any other purpose. When a taxpayer collects (or withholds) a trust amount, the CRA expects that the taxpayer treat these amounts as a sacred trust. In the view of the CRA, a trust debt should be set aside in a separate bank account and never touched, even if the taxpayer has a cash crisis such as an essential supplier bill or payroll due. The CRA would rather that the company ceases to operate or loses the employees than see the company use any trust amounts to keep operating.

With respect to collections action, trust debts are different from other tax debts in two important respects:

- Although the taxpayer can object to an assessment that is related to a trust debt, the collection of that debt does not stop while the objection or tax court appeal is being heard. The government wants the taxpayer to hand over the trust amount while the matter is being determined. After all, the taxpayer collected it for the government.

- If the amount being collected is a trust amount, the CRA's attitude to the collection of the debt will be more severe. The CRA will be less patient in its collection of the debt, and more severe measures will be taken earlier in the process in order to collect the amount.

6. Objections, Tax Court Appeals, and Collections

Any initial Notice of Assessment or Reassessment issued by the CRA can be objected to by filing a Notice of Objection, in the form of a letter and completed T400A form, submitted to the office of the Chief of Appeals. A Notice of Assessment or Reassessment that is adjusted by an appeals officer results in a special notice of reassessment that cannot be objected to via the objection process, but may be appealed to the Tax Court of Canada.

An objection that is rejected completely by an appeals officer results in the issuance of a Notice of Confirmation of the original assessment or reassessment, and may be appealed to the Tax Court of Canada. Appeals to the Tax Court of Canada may only be made after an objection has been filed and processed by an appeals officer, resulting in either a modified Notice of Reassessment or a Notice of Confirmation of the original assessment or reassessment.

An objection should be made within 90 days of a Notice of Assessment or Reassessment. The *Income Tax Act* and the *Excise Tax Act* allow for a grace period of one year from the date in which an objection must be filed. In practice, if you request an extension of time when you file an objection, and it is no more than 90 days plus one year after the date of the Notice of Assessment or Reassessment, it may be accepted for consideration by the office of the Chief of Appeals.

Appeals to the Tax Court of Canada following a modified Notice of Reassessment or Notice of Confirmation after an objection is considered by an appeals officer, and should be made within 90 days of the date of the notice. The Tax Court of Canada also allows for a grace period of one year in addition to the 90-day filing period. However, the acceptance of a late filing requires the consent of the other party, the Department of Justice representing the Crown in right of Canada. It is important that appeals to the Tax Court are done in a timely fashion.

An objection or a subsequent appeal to the Tax Court of Canada generally suspends the collection of a tax debt and other steps to secure the debt, such as the obtaining of a certificate of debt or liens against real estate, unless the objection concerns a trust amount. An objection to an assessment concerning a trust amount will be considered and processed in the same manner as would a non-trust amount; however, collection of the debt will not stop. A taxpayer in such a situation is best served by repaying the amount under protest, challenging the debt with an objection, and hoping for a win and refund via the objection or tax court processes.

There are certain circumstances in which the CRA will not wait 90 days before taking actions to secure a debt, even for non-trust amounts. See section 7.4, Jeopardy Orders, later in this chapter for more information.

If you make a late objection with a request for an extension of time, and the objection is accepted, some steps taken by the agency prior to the filing of the objection will not be reversed, even if the objection concerns a non-trust amount. For example, if a certificate of debt was obtained by the agency in federal court prior to the filing of the objection, the certificate will stay in place. Similarly, liens against property and vehicle titles will also stay in place. However, short-term collection measures such as garnishment of pay, trade receivables, or bank accounts via requirement to pay orders, will be withdrawn by the collections officer if the amount in dispute concerns a regular T1 (personal) or T2 (corporate) tax debt and not a trust amount such as GST, HST, payroll, CPP, or EI.

An objection to an assessment or reassessment concerning a regular tax debt will result in the imposition of a "stall code" for the item on the taxpayer's account with the CRA. In practice, this means that collection of the debt stops or is not begun. A collections officer may still contact the taxpayer and advise him or her of the debt, and request that the debt be paid. A collections officer will often encourage a taxpayer to make voluntary payments against a disputed tax debt, noting that interest continues to accumulate on a disputed amount. A collections officer will also point out that if the taxpayer pays a disputed amount, then wins his or her objection, the amount will be refunded with interest. An objection to a non-trust amount will result in a line item appearing as a "disputed amount" on a taxpayer's T1 or T2 statement of account. It will also affect the "undisputed amount owing" line.

The typical delay between the filing of an objection and the assignment of an appeals officer to hear that objection is between 6 and 12 months. An objection that is related to an ongoing court case may be held "in abeyance" by the CRA until the court renders a decision that may inform the CRA's handling of the objection, resulting in delays that can be two years or more.

When an objection is adjudicated by an appeals officer, there are three possible outcomes:

- The objection is upheld completely.
- The objection is upheld in part.
- The objection is rejected and the original Notice of Assessment or Reassessment is confirmed.

In many cases, an objection to an assessment concerns only a portion of that assessment. For example, a disallowed tax shelter may result in the reversal of a deduction as well as the imposition of a penalty. A taxpayer may realize, belatedly, that the deduction was invalid or that the CRA will not grant the deduction.

This taxpayer could object solely to the gross negligence penalties associated with the deduction. An objection can block collections on both the resulting tax owing due to the reversal of the deduction as well as the associated gross negligence penalty. Interest continues to accumulate. If a taxpayer knows he or she will owe an amount due to a reversed deduction or expense, even if he or she wins a positive decision for some other item in dispute, he or she would be well-served by paying that amount in order to stop the accumulation of interest while the matter is pending.

6.1 Frivolity penalty of 10 percent

Although a taxpayer can object to just about anything, objections devoid of content or reasonable grounds can be penalized with a frivolity penalty of 10 percent of the amount of the disputed assessment or reassessment. So while it may be tempting to file an objection in order to temporarily block collections, such an action carries the risk of a financial penalty.

6.2 Diary promises and good faith

The disposition of a collections officer to a taxpayer depends in large part on the taxpayer's history of previous tax compliance. If a taxpayer has made arrangements with the call centre or a collections officer in the past, and he or she has not made promised payments at the scheduled times, a collector will be less patient and less flexible during the collections process.

In addition, if part of a tax debt consists of interest and penalties, there is little point in arguing about them or making a distinction between them and core taxes payable. Unless collections are blocked by an objection, debts due to interest and penalties are collectable. Even if these items are the subject of a pending relief application, the collections officer simply will not care.

6.3 Payment plans

The CRA has three kinds of payment plans:

- Those agreed to by the call centre
- Interim Payment Plans (IPP)
- Final payment plans

Final payment plans, which are binding written agreements, are difficult to obtain. The objective of a taxpayer with a tax debt should be to pay off the debt immediately, or in the event he or she is unable to do so, to negotiate an IPP with the collections officer. Should a taxpayer succeed in negotiating an IPP, the person should bear in mind that such agreements are considered broken if he or she accumulates a new tax debt while paying off the old one. For example, a taxpayer offering to repay $5,000 per month against an old debt should ensure that he or she has sufficient cash flow to honor his or her other tax obligations as they come due.

In some cases, it's wise to negotiate a repayment plan taking all outstanding taxes into account, including amounts that will appear during the course of the agreement, such as quarterly installment payments. Collections officers will resist this. If a taxpayer has multiple collections officers collecting different taxes, he or she can request in writing that the collections be consolidated so that he or she only has to deal with one collections officer.

6.4 The essentials of life

Even if a taxpayer is self-employed or runs a business, the CRA must take into account the effects of collections actions on the family of the entrepreneur. The CRA must consider the need for the provision of the essentials of life for a family, especially one involving minor dependent children or live-in parents. In such cases, it is often effective to voluntarily complete income and expense and net worth sheets, accompanied by a letter explaining that the entrepreneur's family will be denied the essentials of life such as food, clothing, and shelter should collections activities continue. The collections officer will have to respond to such a claim, especially if it was submitted in writing.

6.5 Creators of high-quality employment

The CRA also has an informal policy of considering the effects of collections actions on providers of high-quality employment. This can often be subjective and arbitrary. If an entrepreneur or company owes a large tax debt, but employs a dozen skilled tradespeople or machinists making $30 per hour, the CRA officer may take this into account. If an enterprise only provides marginal employment opportunities, such as minimum wage fast food or warehouse jobs, it may not sway the CRA.

7. CRA Collection Powers

The CRA is given broad powers to collect tax debts. It can and does use them on a regular basis. The following sections discuss the CRA's collection powers.

7.1 Requirement to pay

The *Income Tax Act* and *The Excise Tax Act* empower collections officers to seize money from financial institutions, payroll cheques, and trade receivables. These powers are exercised in the form of letters issued by the collections officers in the name of the Crown in right of Canada, and carry the force of law.

7.1a Bank account seizures

A requirement to pay issued to a bank generally has the effect of freezing withdrawals and emptying the account. For instance, if a taxpayer owes $40,000 and there is $5,000 in his or her bank account, a requirement to pay letter issued to the bank will ask that the current balance and future deposits or electronic transfers be remitted to the CRA until the entire debt of $40,000 is paid.

Some collections officers will pretend that they do not have the power to remove such requirements to pay, or blame the actions on a "supervisor." These assertions by the collections officers are generally mistruths. The collections officers seek to maximize their leverage by applying pressure to the taxpayers. The collections officers have the ability to withdraw a requirement to pay at any time. If taxpayers receive direct deposits into their accounts, they should have those payments changed to a cheques; otherwise, the CRA will simply keep intercepting the deposited monies.

Collections officers will sometimes adopt the position that the requirement to pay will stay in place until the entire debt is satisfied. Some collections officers, despite their daily contact with entrepreneurs, either have a profound lack of understanding of how businesses operate, or pretend not understand. At this point many taxpayers turn to a professional representative to apply the necessary pressure to remove the requirement to pay.

7.1b Seizure of trade receivables

A trade receivable, such as a payment from a client, can be intercepted by the CRA by the issuance of a Requirement to Pay letter. This is generally not good marketing for the entrepreneur, and can cause him or her to lose some or all of his or her clients. The difficulty with a trade receivable requirement to pay is that it intercepts all of the monies in a transaction. Collections officers will often assert that a requirement to pay must be 100 percent or nothing. This is a mistruth because collections officers can specify that a requirement to pay be set at 50 percent or even less.

A person or company receiving a requirement to pay must cooperate. Failure to respect a requirement to pay makes that person or company responsible for the amount they failed to remit as demanded by the requirement to pay letter.

7.1c Payroll garnishment

A taxpayer who is paid as a payroll employee does not usually have the same kinds of tax problems as a self-employed person or business. However, some entrepreneurs give up their business, become an employee of another company, and then have their tax problems follow them to their new place of employment. The only good news in such a situation is that the requirement to pay is generally set at 30 percent of the post-tax amount of the paycheque, unless the taxpayer is a high earner, at which point the requirement to pay could be set as high as 50 percent.

Employees are protected by legislation in most provinces from being disciplined or dismissed due to a requirement to pay attaching part of their paycheque.

7.2 Certificates of debt and liens

In cases where a taxpayer has a debt of $20,000 or more, or where there is a debt which the taxpayer does not seem to be paying down to the CRA's satisfaction, the CRA may seek a surety (security) by seeking a certificate of debt in Federal Court, and by imposing a lien on real estate or vehicles. These liens go on the property title, and in the case where a property or an asset is sold (or when the property or asset is forcefully sold by the CRA), the liens are paid out to the CRA after the first mortgage, second mortgage, and any other liens which predated the CRA liens are paid out. These liens are not typically lifted until a debt is paid. Sometimes there is enough equity in the property or asset such that the CRA gets the full amount of the taxes owed. In other cases, after the mortgages are paid out, there is not enough equity left to pay the CRA. In such cases, the CRA will take the amount it is given and will still pursue the taxpayer for the remainder.

Note that if a taxpayer wants to refinance his or her property, the bank will not want to be behind the Crown on a deed. In such cases, the CRA can issue a "letter of postponement," in which it agrees to put what remains of the debt owed to the CRA as a lien after the second mortgage obtained in the refinancing. Such letters of postponement are rare, and some collections officers may not have heard of them or will pretend not to have heard of them. Generally the CRA will expect that the lion's share of the refinancing monies is remitted to the Receiver General at the time of closing of the financing round.

In some provinces, a lien document may be called a Notice of Seizure and Sale. It is important to seek advice to determine whether a document is simply a lien or refers to actual impending seizure and sale actions.

7.3 Asset seizures

Asset seizures involve the services of a bailiff or sheriff, typically after 30 days' notice, to enforce a certificate of debt or lien. This generally represents a complete breakdown in the relationship between the collections officer and the taxpayer or company owing taxes.

If you receive a notice from a bailiff or sheriff, challenge it in writing immediately. This will give your lawyer or representative time to negotiate one last time, often with the Department of Justice representing the CRA.

7.4 Jeopardy orders

A large assessment or reassessment, which may be greater than the net worth of a taxpayer or business, may cause the CRA to seek an emergency jeopardy order from the Court of Queen's Bench or Superior Court, depending on the province or territory in which the taxpayer resides. Such emergency orders generally allow for the issuance of a certificate of debt and liens against properties and vehicles to secure the assets, even before the end of the 90-day period, and even after the filing of an objection by the taxpayer. These steps are also taken in extraordinary circumstances such as when a taxpayer has substantial ties to another jurisdiction or is viewed as someone who may flee and try to liquidate assets before the CRA and the courts can consider a tax matter.

7.5 Section 227: Director's liability assessments

Although the purpose of incorporation is to create a shield between the company's creditor's and the personal assets of its principals, certain tax debts can be attached personally to the directors of a company. Trust amounts such as GST, CPP, and EI owed by the company can be assessed as personal debts of the directors in certain circumstances.

In legal terms, the directors of a company have a duty of care to ensure that trust debts are paid, which makes them personally liable. In practice, the CRA views directors as guarantors of the debt, despite being reproached for this view by many tax court judges. Before a director can be personally assessed for a corporation's trust amount debts, the ability of the corporation to pay must first be exhausted. If the collections officer then assesses the director personally, this can be objected to and even appealed in tax court. However, it is very difficult to escape director's liability if the person has been a director of a company in the previous two years.

7.6 Section 160: Assessments for non-arm's length capital transfer

A person or company with a tax debt, whether it is assessed or not, may not transfer capital to non-arm's length parties at the time the person or company has a tax debt. This can take many forms, such as transferring cash to adult children, selling a cottage to a brother-in-law for less than market price, or transferring the share of a house to a spouse. In such cases a collector will send a letter to the person who received those monies and inform him or her that he or she must remit the monies to the CRA. If a taxpayer is in trouble and he or she transfers assets to his or her spouse and other family members, the taxpayer is dragging those people into his or her troubles.

A more exotic interpretation of the section 160 rule concerns dividends and asset stripping. Many small companies pay their principals by dividend rather than payroll. If a company owes a tax debt, any monies remitted to the principal as dividends or management fees will be deemed as "asset stripping." This allows collections officers to treat T2 corporate taxes payable as essentially another form of trust debt which attaches to the principal. Monies received via a payroll are not considered asset stripping and are not subject to section 160.

7.7 Notional assessments: GST and payroll

If a taxpayer or company fails to file GST or payroll reports, the CRA may use information on hand or requested from financial institutions to estimate the debt in the form of a Notional Assessment. This assessment is a legal debt, although it can be reduced or eliminated by an actual filing if this is done within the statutory four-year period.

7.8 Arbitrary assessment office memo: T1 and T2

If a taxpayer or company fails to file T1 or T2 income tax returns, the CRA may use information on hand or requested from financial institutions to estimate the debt in the form of an Arbitrary Assessment. This assessment is a legal debt, although it can be reduced or eliminated by an actual filing if this is done within the statutory ten- or four-year period, for T1 and T2 debts respectively.

12
BANKRUPTCY AND YOUR TAXES

Many taxpayers in Canada get to the point with the collections department where their business has been shut down, or where they are not given the opportunity to pay out the debt over enough time to make repayment possible. In these cases, assets become seized, houses are lost, and oftentimes taxpayers have to avail themselves of the bankruptcy system in order to make the remainder of their tax debts disappear. It is unfortunate that in most cases where taxpayers declare bankruptcy primarily due to tax debts, it would have been the preference of the taxpayers to have been given some relief and a reasonable payment plan. Most taxpayers do not wish to declare bankruptcy to erase tax debts, and do so only as a last option.

In Canada, bankruptcy, can be filed when a person or a company with at least $1,000 in debt becomes insolvent and cannot pay the debts as they become due. Governed by the *Bankruptcy and Insolvency Act*, bankruptcy is a process which can be employed both by individuals and businesses in order to address the debts and get a fresh start. The office of the Superintendent of Bankruptcy, oversees the administration of the system and the federally licensed trustees who work on behalf of the creditors of the bankrupt.

In 2006, there were 98,450 personal insolvency filings in Canada: 79,218 bankruptcies and 19,232 consumer proposals.

Note: As this is not a text on bankruptcy, and since the author is not an expert in the field, this chapter is not intended to be instructive on the mechanics and intricacies of Canadian bankruptcy laws. As such, to find out if declaring bankruptcy is right for you, you should speak to a trustee.

1. Discharge of Taxes in Bankruptcy

Not all debts can be discharged through a bankruptcy, such as secured debts, child support debts, alimony, and certain student loan debts. Luckily for Canadian taxpayers, bankruptcy does allow the discharge of unsecured debts, which include taxes, personal loans, credit cards, and other debt.

As this chapter includes very general information for the average Canadian reader, it provides information in general terms, and if you are considering bankruptcy, you should consult with a trustee in order to determine which debts can and cannot be discharged through a bankruptcy.

The following are some debts that will not be discharged by bankruptcy:

- Student loans less than ten years old

- Child support

- Spousal support

- Fines and most court ordered restitution payments

- Debts that arose as a result of fraud or theft

- Certain government overpayments

The following are some debts that could be discharged by bankruptcy:

- Credit card debt

- Unsecured lines of credit and loans

- Income taxes

- Utility bills

- Past due insurance premiums

- Payday loans

2. Advantages and Disadvantages of Bankruptcy

The benefits of bankruptcy are obvious. Many debts vanish as if by magic! As an added benefit, the collections agents stop calling and the bailiffs stop coming around. Life becomes tolerable again and the taxpayer is allowed to get on with his or her life.

However, bankruptcy is not all magic and fairy tales. It has its downside, and for many, the filing of bankruptcy is a very difficult decision. For taxpayers who hold certain types of licences in the financial sector especially, a bankruptcy is not even an option. In many cases these types of individuals can lose their licences to earn an income in their field.

The following are the advantages of filing for bankruptcy:

- Protects against collection action

- Eliminates certain debts

- Quick process

- Provides a fresh start

The following are the disadvantages of filing for bankruptcy:

- Very damaging to credit history

- Can lose one's possessions and home

- Social stigma

- Some of the debts might not be discharged

- Possible restrictions against running for office or holding certain positions

- Bankruptcy can be costly. Surplus income adds to the cost of bankruptcy. In a bankruptcy, the person may be required to pay to the trustee, which in turn pays the creditors of the bankrupt a percentage of his or her income which exceeds the base amount he or she is allowed to keep in order to pay for his or her personal expenses. This extra income is called the "surplus," and the greater the surplus, the greater the amount that the bankrupt individual will have to pay to the creditors.

• Possibility of losing certain licences; for example, when an individual has licences to sell real estate, insurance, or stocks and bonds, his or her governing body may revoke his or her licence after a bankruptcy.

13
CRIMINAL INVESTIGATIONS

While most Canada Revenue Agency (CRA) audits and investigations aim to assess additional taxes and apply financial penalties, the mandate of the Criminal Investigations Program is to investigate suspected cases of tax evasion, fraud, and other serious violations of tax laws. The difference is that the latter can lead to the laying of criminal charges against a taxpayer.

Since Canada's tax reporting system is a self-reporting system, there is enormous potential for abuse in terms of fraud and tax evasion, and it appears as though many taxpayers are attempting to take advantage of this. According to the CRA, during 2010 to 2011, 129 income tax and GST and HST investigations were referred to the Public Prosecution Service of Canada (PPSC) for prosecution, with an additional 149 cases the year before. The prosecution rate is close to 100 percent, so as you can see, the CRA almost always wins its cases.

Referrals to the PPSC in 2010 to 2011 relating to a tax loss of $25.4 million resulted in 204 convictions for tax evasion or fraud with court-imposed fines of $22.8 million and 47.08 years of jail sentences. In 100 percent of all cases prosecuted, they resulted in convictions, which are publicized on the CRA's website in the Media Centre, as well as in mainstream media and newspapers.

When convicted of tax evasion, providing false statements, failing to file returns, or refusing to comply with CRA requirements, a taxpayer can expect to have court-imposed fines, possible jail time, and still be required to pay penalties and interest to the CRA. If the CRA does not yet know about the false statement or failure, a taxpayer can come forward through the Voluntary Disclosures Program and avoid prosecution and the application of civil penalties. For taxpayers in this position, it is recommended that they seek the advice of a tax lawyer in order to proceed with such a disclosure. If not done properly, the taxpayer may still be prosecuted based on information provided to the CRA. (See Chapter 10 for more information.)

There are many reasons why taxpayers may be charged for tax violations, and most of these relate to fraud in some way or another. From stolen identities used to set up shop and commit GST fraud to the filing of tax returns fraudulently in order to achieve a tax benefit (i.e., tax evasion), many Canadians commit these offences annually and many have to go to criminal court to mount a defence.

There are many types of transgressions which could be considered tax evasion. From the most obvious example of taxpayers hiding income and failing to declare it to the claiming of elevated or fraudulent expenses or charitable donations, taxpayers can expect that such transgressions could be uncovered during an investigation and if so, prosecution can ensue. Some believe that overstating their expenses is not wrong but these taxpayers do not realize that under the law, such an overstatement is the very same thing as hiding income.

The bottom line is the fact that any deliberate attempt to reduce a taxpayer's tax owing by manipulating numbers and providing incorrect information on a return is a serious offence and is grounds for a criminal prosecution.

1. CRA Criminal Investigation Procedures

While the CRA has broad authority to conduct audits and investigations to ensure compliance with the taxation system, it is important to ensure that the CRA does not abuse its powers to collect information during an audit which is actually going be used in a criminal case against the taxpayer. Sometimes an auditor suspects criminal activity and before transferring the file to a criminal investigator or informing the taxpayer that he or she is being investigated criminally, the auditor may try to collect information which would be used as evidence against the person in a criminal proceeding.

1.1 The start of an investigation

Taxpayers don't always know when they are the subject of a criminal investigation, and may not know until they are contacted by a criminal investigator or have agents show up at their premises with police in order to execute a search warrant.

Since there are certain protections under the Canadian Charter of Rights and Freedoms available to a taxpayer who is being investigated criminally, it is essential at all stages to know the purpose of the CRA's investigation. Once the predominant purpose of the investigation becomes criminal, the taxpayer need not comply with the CRA's auditors or investigators. Since there is oftentimes a fine line between a regulatory and criminal investigation it is important to be very careful and diligent about determining the purpose of any CRA request.

If there is doubt, the taxpayer can always ask the auditor or investigator the purpose of his or her request. The taxpayer should consult a lawyer in the case that he or she believes there is a criminal purpose for an investigation.

While the auditors and investigators may not come forward to advise the taxpayer that there is a criminal purpose to an investigation, there are some warning signs that can alert the taxpayer to this possibility. Sometimes an auditor will abruptly stop working on a file and a taxpayer may not hear from him or her. It is possible in such cases that the auditor is making a referral to the criminal investigations department. Further, if a taxpayer has been sent correspondence which indicates that there may be possible prosecution if certain documents are not provided or if certain filings are not done, a taxpayer may reasonably expect that he or she could be the subject of a criminal investigation.

During the investigation, an investigator will use all the tools available in order to see if the case is worth pursuing and whether there is a likelihood of a conviction. If there are grounds for the auditor or investigator to believe that a conviction is possible, he or she can obtain credit reports and information from financial institutions, and he or she can start looking into a taxpayers' background — including a previous criminal record. Further, criminal investigators can use surveillance in order to evaluate a case.

There are a number of indicators which can help a taxpayer determine whether in the course of its investigation, the CRA has crossed the line between a regulatory and a criminal investigation. None of these is necessarily proof that an investigation is criminal, but if these indicators are present, they are a good indication that the taxpayer should be suspicious of the CRA's intentions. The following are examples of indicators of a criminal investigation:

- The taxpayer has committed an offence, and based on the knowledge that the CRA or the investigator already has, the taxpayer believes that there may be reasonable grounds to lay charges, or reasonable grounds for the CRA to be suspicious enough to pursue a criminal investigation.

- The auditor or investigator has been asking the type of questions which appear to indicate that he or she is suspicious of possible fraudulent activity on the part of the taxpayer.

- The audit abruptly stops without being completed and a new officer from the CRA contacts the taxpayer to continue.

- The evidence sought by the CRA relates to the taxpayer's guilt rather than the actual numbers involved. For example, if the CRA wants to see emails that were written between a taxpayer and his or her business partner, and not just examine the books, there may be a criminal purpose in mind.

If you suspect a criminal purpose is behind a request for certain information, you should contact a lawyer immediately before complying with a request to provide incriminating information. However, the CRA may still be able to obtain a search warrant to examine or seize the evidence in question.

1.2 Search warrants

Once a determination has been made by the CRA that a conviction is a real possibility, it needs to gather evidence. This is often done by obtaining a warrant to search a taxpayer's home or business, which is obtained without the knowledge of the taxpayer and is obtained after an investigator swears under oath that he or she has reason to believe that evidence exists which could be used to prove a criminal case against a taxpayer.

If a search warrant has been used to obtain information from a taxpayer, it is important that the taxpayer's lawyer examine the warrant to determine if there is any basis under which to challenge the warrant. Sometimes based on errors on the warrant, or problems with the sworn statement of the investigator, a taxpayer's lawyer may successfully mount a challenge and may even have the evidence thrown out or have the charges withdrawn. While challenges are being mounted against search warrants, it is possible to have the evidence obtained from a search sealed and made unavailable to the investigators until such time as the challenge is completed.

1.3 Informants

In order to facilitate the investigation and prosecution in cases where Canada's tax laws have been abused, the CRA maintains an Informant Leads Program, the mandate of which is to "coordinate all leads that the CRA receives from informants, to determine if there is an element of noncompliance with tax legislation, and ensure that the information is reviewed and provided to the corresponding compliance program for appropriate enforcement action."

In short, the program provides a snitch line which can be called in order to provide anonymous tips about suspected tax evasion by Canadian taxpayers.

Besides the snitch line, there are all sorts of ways in which the CRA receives information about a taxpayer which could cause a criminal investigation to ensue. As outlined in Chapter 1, section 2., the CRA is provided with information about a taxpayer from a variety of sources, and some of this information may be used to proceed with criminal investigations. Included in these sources of information are government agencies, police departments, and financial institutions.

2. Charges Resulting from Criminal Investigations

During the course of a criminal investigation the CRA uses all the tools at its disposal in order to build its theory of the case. During this time the CRA does not provide much information to the taxpayer, who may not even know that he or she is being investigated. In cases where a search warrant is executed, the taxpayer has the right to see the information which was sworn in order to obtain the warrant.

When the CRA has developed its theory of the case and has enough evidence to find a taxpayer guilty in court, it will refer the case to the Public Prosecution Service of Canada for charges to be laid against the taxpayer in Provincial Court.

In many cases when taxpayers are charged, they make guilty pleas in return for reduced fines or charges. Since this route also avoids the need for a trial, these taxpayers may also save money on legal fees. In other cases, taxpayers choose to go to trial.

Regardless of whether or not a taxpayer may ultimately want to make a plea arrangement with the Crown prosecutor, it is advisable to consult a lawyer as soon as he or she learns that charges may be laid. In either case, a lawyer may recommend that the taxpayer not cooperate with an ongoing investigation and instead wait for the charges to be laid. At that point the prosecutor would have to provide full disclosure of his or her evidence including all CRA paperwork which he or she intends to use against the taxpayer. By having all of the information, a taxpayer and his or her lawyer are better equipped to determine their strategy. Keeping this in mind, a taxpayer should also realize that his or her best strategy may be to retain a lawyer early on in the process in order to start mounting a defence as soon as possible. With a lawyer on board, a taxpayer can challenge search warrants and may be able to prevent incriminating evidence from landing on the CRA investigator's desk. In many circumstances, the taxpayer may even be able to prevent the CRA from being able to develop a case sufficient for prosecution.

3. Taxpayer Rights during the Criminal Investigation

Once the CRA commences a criminal investigation into the affairs of a taxpayer, it must act in accordance with the Canadian Charter of Rights and Freedoms, which is part of the Canadian Constitution, and guarantees certain rights which are useful in the context of a criminal investigation.

Most importantly the Charter provides the right against self-incrimination and against an unreasonable search and seizure. Because of these Charter rights, the CRA's powers are diminished during a criminal investigation. During a criminal investigation the agency cannot compel a taxpayer to comply with its requests for information. The fact that an investigation is criminal automatically triggers the right to remain silent and to be secure against unreasonable search and seizure.

The CRA is also required to provide taxpayers with certain protections in the case of a criminal investigation. Taxpayers should be informed that an investigation is criminal, they have the right to remain silent, and they have the right to counsel. Further, while the CRA is not required to produce a warrant to examine documents in the course of an audit, it is required to obtain a warrant in the case of a criminal investigation.

14
FIGHT THE CRA IN COURT

While it may be difficult to convince the Canada Revenue Agency (CRA) that the taxpayer's position is correct, and while the CRA may insist that its interpretation of the law is correct, it is nice to know that the CRA does not have the final say and that a federal judge may find otherwise. As a check and balance to the Canadian tax system in which the CRA is provided with an enormous amount of power and discretion to apply the law, a taxpayer may apply to the Tax Court of Canada or to the Federal Court to make a determination as to whether the CRA was correct.

Cases in which it must be determined whether the CRA's interpretation of the law was correct or whether the figures provided by the CRA on Notices of Assessment were accurate, must be brought before the Tax Court of Canada. Cases where it must be determined whether the CRA exercised its discretion properly under the law must be brought before the Federal Court.

1. The Tax Court of Canada

If an objection to a Notice of Assessment or Reassessment has not resulted in a satisfactory outcome for a taxpayer, the only option he or she has to change the amount of tax that is owed is to file an appeal to the Tax Court of Canada. Unlike the filing of an application for taxpayer relief, which may only result in a decrease of interest and penalties, an application to the Tax Court of Canada can result in the reduction of interest and penalties as well as the principal tax amount. If a satisfactory result is not reached in the Tax Court, a taxpayer can appeal to the Federal Court of Appeals, and possibly to the Supreme Court of Canada after that.

Established in 1983 by the *Tax Court of Canada Act*, the Tax Court of Canada is a federal court dealing with tax matters for both individuals and businesses, and it has two different means by which a taxpayer can object. For matters less than $12,000, taxpayers have the option of applying to the court under the simpler, informal procedure, while matters of a greater pecuniary value would be heard under the general procedure. (See Table 1.)

In order to apply under the informal procedure, a taxpayer must elect to use the informal procedure rather than the general procedure by using the election form (see Sample 3). Since it is less formalistic, most self-represented taxpayers choose the informal route when the amount in question is $12,000 or less. Even some taxpayers who have more than $12,000 in question still choose to go the informal way since they can navigate it more easily on their own. They simply have to acknowledge that they will be limited to a $12,000 amount (or $24,000 when a loss is being considered). The only exceptions to this monetary limit are for GST, *Excise Tax Act*, and *Customs Act*, which are all heard under the informal procedure without a limit.

TABLE 1
INFORMAL PROCEDURE VS. GENERAL PROCEDURE

In 2010, of the 3,255 cases heard by the Tax Court, 1,381 were heard under the general procedure with 1,874 cases heard under the informal procedure.

Informal	General
Limit of $12,000	No limit
No lawyer needed	Lawyer required for corporations
Simpler procedure	Formalistic procedure
GST, *Excise Tax Act*, *Customs Act* heard in the informal procedure regardless of limit	

Both the general and the informal procedures are commenced by the filing of a Notice of Appeal to the court. In the Notice of Appeal, the taxpayer is required to indicate the assessment(s) with which he or she disagrees and the issue at hand. The taxpayer is also required to present his or her arguments. Once the paperwork has been filed with the court, a lawyer from the Department of Justice is appointed to represent the CRA, and will soon issue a reply to the Notice of Appeal.

The parties have to exchange documents, can perform an examination, and can interview witnesses. Note that the taxpayer may only interview one witness from the CRA. Following discovery, the matter may be set down for trial, or negotiations may occur between the parties in order to reach a settlement. When cases do go to trial, most matters that are not particularly complex are resolved in a day or less. Certain other matters may take weeks to try in court. At the completion of a trial the judge may or may not render his or her decision, and it is not at all uncommon to have to wait weeks or months for a written decision to be provided.

SCHEDULE 17(3)

ELECTION LIMITING AMOUNTS IN ISSUE
(INFORMAL PROCEDURE)
(SUBSECTION 17(3))

TAX COURT OF CANADA

BETWEEN:

(name)
Appellant,

and

HER MAJESTY THE QUEEN,

Respondent.

<u>ELECTION AND WAIVER</u>

I ELECT to have the informal procedure under the Act apply to this appeal and for this purpose I elect, in accordance with section 17, to limit the appeal to $12,000 as being the aggregate of all amounts in issue in this appeal or, where the amount in issue is a loss, to limit the amount of that loss to $24,000.

Date:

TO: The Registrar
       Tax Court of Canada
       200 Kent Street
       Ottawa, Ontario
       K1A 0M1
or

       Any other office of the Registry.

(Set out name, address for service and telephone number of appellant, appellant's counsel or appellant's agent)

A judge of the Tax Court of Canada has broad discretion as to what type of decision he or she can render. If the matter is found partially or fully in favour of the taxpayer, the judge may require that the CRA issue a reassessment as outlined, or he or she may require the CRA to vacate a reassessment completely when it has no merit at all.

Depending on which party wins the case in court, the judge may award costs to the winning party. Note that if a person brings a frivolous case to court in an effort to stall the CRA's collections, if he or she loses the case, the person may have to pay some of the costs to the CRA as a result.

During an appeal to the Tax Court of Canada, in most circumstances the onus is on the part of the taxpayers to prove their case. The taxpayers can do this by backing up their case with proof, and by disproving assumptions relied on by the CRA. Only in special situations (e.g., the application of certain penalties) where there is a reverse-onus does the CRA have to prove its case and, in order to win, the CRA must prove its case on the balance of probabilities.

For those cases where a settlement is possible, the taxpayer's lawyer will generally negotiate terms of a settlement based on the evidence that has already come forward during discovery. In general, unless the CRA's case is bulletproof, the taxpayer could expect to possibly negotiate a settlement. Frequently it seems that Department of Justice counsel would prefer to avoid having a wasteful trial when a meaningful settlement can be reached instead.

1.1 Informal procedure

The following sections discuss the informal procedure in more detail.

1.1a Filing a Notice of Appeal

Once the taxpayer has prepared his or her Notice of Appeal (see Sample 4), which indicates the assessments involved, and outlines the reasons for the appeal as well as the relevant facts on which the appeal is based, he or she must file it with the court. The taxpayer has the option of doing this in person at the court, by mail or courier, by fax, or on the court's website.

This application has to be made within 90 days of receiving a Notice of Confirmation; if the deadline has passed, the taxpayer must also request an extension in which to file the application, which can be done for up to a one-year period. Note that it is best to make the application in the 90 days allowed in order to avoid having to request the extension.

In order to mount a successful appeal, a taxpayer must have grounds founded in law for his or her case. That means that the law must be on the taxpayer's side — the Tax Court will not rule on grounds of fairness or a sob story.

Similarly, in order to succeed, a taxpayer will have to be able to prove his or her position by providing all necessary evidence and testimony. The better the proof and documentation of a taxpayer's case, the better the case will be.

Regardless of how a taxpayer prepares his or her Notice of Appeal, and whether the person chooses to use the Schedule 4 form shown in Sample 4, the following information must appear in order for the court to accept the appeal:

- The assessment number (if available) or the tax year(s) for which the individual is appealing.

- Date of reassessment or confirmation.

- Taxpayer's identity.

SAMPLE 4
INFORMAL PROCEDURE: NOTICE OF APPEAL

SCHEDULE 4
(Section 4)

NOTICE OF APPEAL (INFORMAL PROCEDURE)

TAX COURT OF CANADA

BETWEEN:
(name)
Appellant,
And

HER MAJESTY THE QUEEN,

Respondent.

<u>NOTICE OF APPEAL</u>

TAKE NOTICE THAT *(name)* appeals to the Court from *(identify the assessment(s) (which include(s) a determination, a redetermination, a reassessment and an additional assessment) under appeal, including date of the assessment(s) and taxation year(s))*, or from the suspension, pursuant to subsection 188.2(2) of the *Income Tax Act*, of its authority to issue an official receipt referred to in Part XXXV of the *Income Tax Regulations*.

A. Reasons for the appeal. *(Here state why you say the assessment(s) or suspension is (are) wrong.)*

B. Statement of relevant facts in support of the appeal.

I ELECT to have the informal procedure provided by sections 18.1 to 18.28 of the *Tax Court of Canada Act* apply to this appeal.

Date:

TO: The Registrar
Tax Court of Canada
200 Kent Street
Ottawa, Ontario
K1A 0M1
or

Any other office of the Registry.

(Set out name, address for service and telephone number of appellant, appellant's counsel or appellant's agent)

NOTE that if the aggregate of all amounts in issue exceeds $12,000, or the amount of loss in issue exceeds $24,000, and you wish to proceed under the informal procedure, you must use Schedule 17(2).

- Complete contact information including telephone and fax numbers (if available).

- Complete contact information for taxpayer's lawyer or agent.

- The grounds for the appeal.

- A statement that the taxpayer is limiting the amount of the appeal to $12,000 for each tax year being appealed (or the taxpayer could file an election limiting amounts in issue — see Sample 3).

- The date of the appeal.

- Taxpayer's signature or representative's signature if a corporation.

1.1b After the Notice of Appeal is filed

After the court has received an appellant's (i.e., the taxpayer) Notice of Appeal, it will issue an acknowledgment. Shortly after, the CRA prepares a reply to the Notice of Appeal, which according to rule 6(1) of the Tax Court of Canada Rules (informal procedure), must include the following:

- The facts that are admitted.

- The facts that are denied.

- The facts of which the respondent has no knowledge and puts in issue.

- The findings or assumptions of fact made by the Minister when making the assessment.

- Any other material facts.

- The issues to be decided.

- The statutory provisions relied on.

- The reasons the respondent intends to rely on.

- The relief sought.

This reply outlines the case that the CRA will be making in the course of the trial, and provides the taxpayer and his or her representative with a good indication of how they must build their case — including what facts and assumptions they have to challenge, as well as what sections of the relevant law is being used to make the respondent's (i.e., the CRA) case.

After the appellant has received the reply, within six months the court will issue a Notice of Hearing providing a time and place for the matter to be heard. These dates should be respected and, outside of extraordinary circumstances, a taxpayer should not take for granted that he or she may be able to obtain an adjournment. Instead a taxpayer may lose his or her opportunity to have the matter heard. It is at this hearing that both parties appear before a judge and present their cases. Frequently a decision is reached the same day.

1.1c Important preparation for the self-represented

For the do-it-yourselfer, the person may wish to get educated about the rules and procedures governing the informal procedure. Much of what is needed with respect to the rules and the technicalities can be found at the website of the Tax Court of Canada (www.tcc-cci.gc.ca), including links to the Department of Justice's site in order to find the Tax Court of Canada Rules (informal procedure) in PDF form.

Furthermore, the self-represented needs to be able to prove that his or her case has a legal foundation. Careful review of the *Income Tax Act* or *Excise Tax Act* and the relevant regulations is necessary in order to be able to file an effective Notice of Appeal and to defend his or her case against the CRA who are always well prepared.

Additional sources of information which may help in the preparation of your case and which may help you understand your issue more thoroughly are documents prepared by the CRA including tax bulletins and information circulars. These highlight the CRA's policies and its interpretation of the law.

It may be helpful to research cases that were similar to yours in order to prove your case. If something worked in another case, maybe it will work for yours. Plus, if the other case arguments were convincing to the court previously, referencing that particular case may be convincing to the court in your case. In other words, there may be some precedential value to the other case. However, be careful of other cases which were heard under the informal procedure. According to the *Tax Court of Canada Act*, judgments under the informal procedure have no precedential value for any other case in the Tax Court of Canada (see section 18.28 of the act).

1.2 General procedure

Since it is far more complicated, most taxpayers do not choose to represent themselves for cases being heard under the general procedure and instead engage the services of a tax lawyer or another representative. Hiring a lawyer is usually for the best when it comes to general procedure matters. For a corporation, unless it has received permission of the court to allow an officer to represent it, there is no choice but to engage a lawyer as its representative.

For those who still insist on self-representing, they are well advised to become very knowledgeable about all the rules governing the general procedure. Similarly, if the person chooses to hire a representative who is not a lawyer, the taxpayer should have a high comfort level about that individual's ability to argue a case in court as well as his or her knowledge of all the rules and procedures involved in getting to court. At the end of the day, whoever is chosen to represent the taxpayer will be arguing against a lawyer from the Department of Justice who has done this many times before, and who will

be well prepared and knowledgeable in every aspect of the case and of court procedure.

1.2a Filing a Notice of Appeal

Rule 21 of the Tax Court of Canada Rules (general procedure) dictates the form of an appeal to the court according to the type of proceeding. For example, an appeal from an assessment under the *Income Tax Act* or the *Excise Tax Act* would require the use of form 21(1)(a), while an appeal from a determination of the fair market value of an object by the Canadian Cultural Property Export Review Board would require form 21(1)(d).

Unlike the informal procedure, the general procedure is very specific about many details. In order to navigate the system, an appellant must know exactly what is expected of him or her and when.

1.2b After the Notice of Appeal is filed

One major difference between the informal and the general process is that a lawyer from the Department of Justice will be representing the CRA in court. As such, once the appeal has been received by the court, a copy is forwarded to the Department of Justice where a lawyer is assigned to the case.

With help from his or her client, the CRA, the Department of Justice lawyer prepares the reply to the Notice of Appeal filed on behalf of the appellant. In turn, should the appellant decide to do so, he or she may answer the reply within 30 days. This is not a necessary step.

Once the pleadings have been completed, the parties to the case are required to exchange the documents on which they will be relying to prove their case. Following the production of the documents, the parties will engage in either written or live examinations for discovery in which they will be able to ask questions of the other party.

GENERAL PROCEDURES: NOTICE OF APPEAL

FORM 21(1)(a)

NOTICE OF APPEAL — GENERAL PROCEDURE

TAX COURT OF CANADA

BETWEEN:
(name)
Appellant,
and

HER MAJESTY THE QUEEN,
Respondent.

NOTICE OF APPEAL

(a) In the case of an individual, state home address in full; and in the case of a corporation, state address in full of principal place of business in the province in which the appeal is being instituted;

(b) Identify the assessment(s) under appeal: include date of assessment(s) and, if the appeal is under the Income Tax Act, include taxation year(s) or, if the appeal is under the *Excise Tax Act*, the *Customs Act*, the *Air Travellers Security Charge Act*, the *Excise Act*, 2001, or the *Softwood Lumber Products Export Charge Act*, 2006, include the period to which the assessment(s) relate(s);

(c) Relate the material facts relied on;

(d) Specify the issues to be decided;

(e) Refer to the statutory provisions relied on;

(f) Set forth the reasons the appellant intends to rely on;

(g) Indicate the relief sought; and

(h) Date of notice.

(Name of appellant or appellant's counsel)

(Address for service, telephone number, fax number, if any, of appellant's counsel or, if appellant is appearing in person, state telephone number or fax number, if any)

The trial is not always necessary, and sometimes may be avoided through negotiation of a settlement with the counsel from the Department of Justice. If a trial is necessary, there are a host of rules which dictate every aspect of the proceeding, including such details as the quality and size of the paper to be used for court documents, as well as the spacing of text and the margins on the side. During the trial, witnesses are called, and each side is permitted to make its case. If the onus is on the taxpayer to make his or her case, he or she will speak first, otherwise opposing counsel will.

After the hearing is complete, the judge will issue a decision, which could take several months to be drafted.

2. Federal Court and Federal Court of Appeal

After the Tax Court of Canada has rendered its decision on a case, the taxpayer can appeal to the Federal Court of Appeal. The appeals court also has very specific rules which govern each aspect of an appeal. One such rule that taxpayers considering an appeal should be aware of, is that an appeal can only be made on the basis that there was an error in law in the Tax Court of Canada decision. An appeal cannot be made on the basis of the facts of the case. If a matter is of national importance, the Supreme Court of Canada may choose to hear the case if unsuccessful at the Federal Court of Appeal.

For certain matters for which the federal government has been given jurisdiction, such as navigation and shipping, intellectual property, national defence, railroads, telecommunications, and tax, the Federal Court and the Federal Court of Appeal have jurisdiction. These courts also have jurisdiction to review all decisions and exercise of discretion of federal tribunals, agencies, commissions, etc. As a rule, anywhere that ministerial (governmental) power is delegated to officials who can exercise their discretion and arrive at a decision, these courts have jurisdiction to review that decision.

While assessments and reassessments can be objected to, and while a failed objection can be appealed to the Tax Court of Canada, certain decisions, such as a denial for taxpayer relief, cannot be objected to. Rather these decisions have to be reviewed by a judge in the Federal Court in the process of judicial review.

While there are a number of registry offices for the Federal Courts, a taxpayer may choose to deal with the office most convenient for him or her. A list of offices is available on the Courts Administration Service's website (www.cas-satj.gc.ca).

2.1 Judicial review

There are many reasons why a taxpayer would go through the process of judicial review. One big reason is to have the court review a denial of a request for taxpayer relief. Imagine the perfect case for relief: The person was in a coma and unable to file his or her returns. What if the person's request for taxpayer relief for the late-filing penalties was denied for no good reason at all — even though the CRA was provided with proof indicating the taxpayer's inability to have filed during the time he or she was in a coma? What if the CRA didn't allow the taxpayer to provide any proof? What if the CRA exercised its discretion to deny the relief in an unfair and unreasonable manner?

When there is a case for judicial review, a judge of the Federal Court can review the exercise of discretion of the CRA to determine whether it was fair and reasonable. If the reason to deny relief for late filing penalties to the taxpayer in a coma was based on the fact that the taxpayer has blue eyes, or is somebody who once stole a car, or somebody who has too many parking tickets, then the decision was not based on the law and could easily be reviewed. In the course of a review, if the court decides the process used to reject the application did not demonstrate a fair and reasonable exercise of the CRA's discretion, the taxpayer can win his or her case and have the CRA go through the process again — fairly this time.

2.1a Process to file an application for judicial review

Applications for judicial review are governed by the Federal Courts Rules (rule 300 to 319) and the *Federal Courts Act* (section 18.1). In order to have a CRA decision reviewed, a taxpayer must complete a Notice of Application, or form 301 (see Sample 6). For more complete information on the steps required to make an application for judicial review, you may consult the document "How to File an Application for Judicial Review" on the website of the Federal Court.

The most important thing to remember with an application for judicial review is that it cannot be late. If a taxpayer receives a decision from the CRA with which he or she disagrees, it is important to consult a tax lawyer as soon as possible in order to determine whether there is a case for judicial review, and in order to go through the process in time. Oftentimes the law only provides up to 30 days in which to file an application for judicial review, and applications filed outside of that period allowed for by law will be rejected unless there is a motion filed in order to request an extension of time.

Once the application is filed with the court, there are many steps to be taken before having the application heard by a judge. Once all the paperwork has been done, all the exchange of documents has taken place, and the parties are ready, the hearing itself is finally requested through a "Requisition for a Hearing" by using form 314 (see Sample 7).

In many cases, a settlement may be reached before the matter is ever heard. If a taxpayer is confident (or cavalier), and chooses to represent himself or herself in a judicial review application, he or she is strongly advised to become familiar with the Federal Court Rules to ensure that he or she does not lose the case based on a technicality or by being late in performing some detail. However, this option of self-representation is not available to companies, associations, and groups of people, which by virtue of rule 120 of the Federal Courts Rules, are all required to be represented by a lawyer.

JUDICIAL REVIEW: NOTICE OF APPLICATION

FORM 301 - Rule 301

NOTICE OF APPLICATION

[General Heading -- Use Form 66]

(Court seal)

NOTICE OF APPLICATION

TO THE RESPONDENT:

A PROCEEDING HAS BEEN COMMENCED by the applicant. The relief claimed by the applicant appears on the following page.

THIS APPLICATION will be heard by the Court at a time and place to be fixed by the Judicial Administrator. Unless the Court orders otherwise, the place of hearing will be as requested by the applicant. The applicant requests that this application be heard at [place where Federal Court of Appeal (or Federal Court) ordinarily sits].

IF YOU WISH TO OPPOSE THIS APPLICATION, to receive notice of any step in the application or to be served with any documents in the application, you or a solicitor acting for you must prepare a notice of appearance in Form 305 prescribed by the Federal Courts Rules and serve it on the applicant's solicitor, or where the applicant is self-represented, on the applicant, WITHIN 10 DAYS after being served with this notice of application.

Copies of the Federal Courts Rules information concerning the local offices of the Court and other necessary information may be obtained on request to the Administrator of this Court at Ottawa (telephone 613-992-4238) or at any local office.

IF YOU FAIL TO OPPOSE THIS APPLICATION, JUDGMENT MAY BE GIVEN IN YOUR ABSENCE AND WITHOUT FURTHER NOTICE TO YOU.

(Date)

Issued by:_____
(Registry Officer)

Address of local office:_____

TO: (Name and address of each respondent)
(Name and address of every other person required to be served)

[Separate page]

APPLICATION

(Where the application is an application for judicial review)

This is an application for judicial review in respect of

(Identify the tribunal)

(Set out the date and details of the decision, order, or other matter in respect of which judicial review is sought.)

The applicant makes application for: (State the precise relief sought.)

The grounds for the application are: (State the grounds to be argued, including any statutory provision or rule relied on.)

This application will be supported by the following material: (List the supporting affidavits, including documentary exhibits, and the portions of transcripts to be used.)

(If the applicant wishes a tribunal to forward material to the Registry, add the following paragraph:)

The applicant requests (name of the tribunal) to send a certified copy of the following material that is not in the possession of the applicant but is in the possession of the (tribunal) to the applicant and to the Registry: (Specify the particular material.)

(Date)

_____
(Signature of solicitor or applicant)
(Name, address, telephone and fax number of solicitor or applicant)

JUDICIAL REVIEW: REQUISITION FOR A HEARING

FORM 314 - Rule 314

REQUISITION FOR HEARING -- APPLICATION

[General Heading -- Use Form 66]

REQUISITION FOR HEARING

THE APPLICANT REQUESTS that a date be set for the hearing of this application.

THE APPLICANT CONFIRMS:

1. The requirements of subsection 309(1) of the Federal Courts Rules have been complied with.

2. A notice of constitutional question has been served in accordance with section 57 of the *Federal Courts Act*.

(or)

There is no requirement to serve a notice of constitutional question under section 57 of the *Federal Courts Act* in this application.

3. The hearing should be held at (place).

4. The hearing should last no longer than (number) hours (or days).

5. The representatives of all parties to the application are as follows:

(a) on behalf of the applicant: (name of solicitor or party if self-represented) who can be reached at: (address, telephone and fax numbers)

(b) on behalf of the respondent: (name of solicitor or party if self-represented) who can be reached at: (address, telephone and fax numbers)

(c) on behalf of the intervener: (name of solicitor or party if self-represented) who can be reached at: (address, telephone and fax numbers)

(If more than one applicant, respondent, or intervener represented by different solicitors, list all.)

6. The parties are available at any time except: (List all dates within the next 90 days on which the parties are not available for a hearing.)

7. The hearing will be in (English or French, or partly in English and partly in French).

(Date)

_____
(Signature of solicitor or applicant)
(Name, address, telephone and fax number of solicitor or applicant)

TO: (Name and address of each solicitor or party served with requisition)

15
TAX SCHEMES

As long as there has been greed and taxes there have been tax schemes and, over the last few years, I have noticed that there have been an increasing number of victims coming out of the woodwork who have all been caught by the Canada Revenue Agency (CRA) for their involvement in one tax scheme or another. Either the percentage of the people who choose to get help has increased, or the number of schemes has increased, or the CRA's ability to compare tax returns and uncover more of these schemes has become better — perhaps all three.

Since the economy has been poor over the last few of years, one would expect to have seen an increase in prevalence of these schemes — particularly since it is during a recession when people are most vulnerable and more eager to want to derive the benefit promised for participation — that benefit is the key to the whole problem.

What all of the tax schemes have in common is that the taxpayers (victims) who participate believe they are going to receive a benefit for their participation. The scheme may be about curing cancer, providing AIDS medicine to people in Africa, vaccinating children, or helping build a church. Taxpayers may be participating thinking they are helping others but they are also participating because they are told that they will receive a higher tax refund than they otherwise would. They would not be participating without the anticipation of that higher refund. They would not donate money to that particular church (which they have never been to), or donate money to that particular Africa mission (which they have never heard of) without the benefit.

The taxpayers are told that the scheme is legitimate and legal. Sometimes charities are involved, and these charities at the time of the scheme, are registered and in good standing with the CRA.

The one commonality of the scams is that they seem to offer a financial benefit for participation. They typically masquerade as a charity and although charitable donations are not usually seen by donors as a way to get a benefit (other than a moral or religious benefit), many of the tax scams will allow the donor to receive more back from the CRA in terms of a refund than they actually gave to the charity in the first place. These scams all target and are perpetuated by the greed of the average Canadian. While there are people who get into these scams unwittingly, and with the true desire to help burn victims or starving children, the majority of contributors to these scams will all admit, at least to themselves, that they knew what they were getting into was "too good to be true." It is when a proposition, especially one that involves the CRA, appears too good to be true, that is a good time to become suspicious of what you are getting involved with.

The increasing number of scams coupled with the CRA's numerous recent campaigns to clamp down on some of the larger and more persistent schemes, has resulted in an enormous number of people, including doctors, teachers, architects, RCMP officers, clergymen, and bus drivers who have cumulatively lost tens if not hundreds of million dollars in these schemes, and who have been left with debts to the CRA that far exceeded what they benefitted from participation in the scheme in the first place. Even worse, some are charged criminally with participation in these scams, while others lose their homes from the severe penalties. The common denominator is that participants of Canadian tax scams can expect the CRA to eventually find them and make their lives a living hell.

Project Trident is one such program that has been designed by the CRA to prosecute key players in fraudulent tax schemes. Project Trident targets tax preparer fraud, charity related fraud, and identity theft, and to date it has been responsible for 822 months in mandatory jail time, and more than $3 million in fines — 114 investigations are ongoing at the time of this book's publication.

There are a variety of consequences of participation in a tax scam or scheme. Even in the best case scenario, and with the best lawyer and the best deal with the CRA, the participant in a tax scam will be out of pocket for lawyer's fees, initial contribution, or the fees paid to the promoter, advisor, or tax return preparer who sold the taxpayer on the scheme in the first place. In other scenarios the consequences range from financial such as penalties and years of accrued interest, to criminal such as charges for participating in, promoting, or being behind a scheme.

There are a number of provisions of the *Income Tax Act* that allow the CRA to penalize taxpayers for their involvement in a tax scam, and taxpayers are always best served by asking their tax accountant or tax lawyer for an opinion before participating in what might be a scam, and by staying clear of any proposed tax scheme which involves receiving a higher benefit than they think they would otherwise deserve. If it seems too good to be true, remember that it most likely is.

Right 11 of the Taxpayer Bill of Rights guarantees that the CRA is accountable. It reads, "You have the right to expect us to be accountable for what we do" Yet they allocate charitable licences and tax shelter identification numbers without much consideration then fail to police and monitor these organizations carefully.

You would not believe how easy it is to start your own charity. If you do so, you could run your own scheme for a while and issue bogus charitable receipts and cook the books and scam a lot of taxpayers before the CRA would even have had the chance to audit you properly. Because the CRA does not police and monitor charities better, you may be lead to think that the CRA has failed taxpayers who are victimized by the charities and tax shelters. To add insult to injury, the CRA goes ahead and reassesses these victims with serious penalties and interest charges.

Right number 14 of the Taxpayer Bill of Rights guarantees Canadian taxpayers the right to expect the CRA to warn you about questionable tax schemes "in a timely manner." This doesn't mean years after a taxpayer has contributed, or years after the CRA already knew about the scam. Timely means soon after the CRA finds out about the scheme. Since the CRA is accountable, timely would also mean that it should be proactive about uncovering a scheme, and should do so in a reasonable time frame.

I have numerous clients who have been involved in tax schemes, and I have spoken to many hundreds more in consultations. Yet in my practice I have never encountered anybody who has ever received any warning about any questionable tax scheme. Their only warning was when they were reassessed or informed that they were being audited or investigated for participation.

In certain cases I have seen that the scheme was ongoing even after certain waves of victims had been investigated and reassessed for their participation. This would indicate that the CRA knew of the scheme, but took insufficient action to warn the public about the scheme, and prevent the scammers from further victimizing taxpayers. While the CRA eventually puts a warning deep within its website,

the public would be better served if the CRA would purchase a giant ad on the front page of all major newspapers across the country each time a scam was uncovered; however, the CRA doesn't do this. It also doesn't do a good job of investigating enough of the scams early enough. It also doesn't do a good job of upholding right number 14 of the Taxpayer Bill of Rights — giving taxpayers timely information regarding questionable tax schemes.

In fact, there are many questionable tax schemes that operate today under the CRA's nose with valid charitable registration numbers and official letterheads and premises. The CRA probably knows about many of them, but for some reason habitually keeps this information to itself for years. Many times before alerting the public, the CRA performs investigations which last for years, after which it publicizes and then reassesses the taxpayers involved. There are many taxpayers who have participated in schemes for multiple years only to be reassessed for all the years after the completion of an investigation. Many such taxpayers unfortunately continued to participate in years which they would never have participated had the CRA informed them after their first year that the tax scheme they had participated in was questionable.

Many Canadians get themselves into trouble for the simple reason that they trust the Charities Directory. The CRA maintains an online listing of all the charities, which can be searched. All too frequently when I do consultations for victims of charity scams, they inform me that they believed that they were doing their due diligence before contributing to a charity simply by checking the charity in the registry, or by calling the CRA and hearing that the charity is registered and in good standing.

All tax scams share certain similarities and are all designed to defraud their victims for as long as possible before they are ultimately shutdown. No matter how they are disguised, and whether they purport to be businesses, charities, or educators, the organizations that perpetuate Canadian tax scams are usually run by sophisticated criminals. The scams are in turn sold to average taxpayers through a network of promoters (usually business advisors, income tax return preparers, or financial planners) who typically receive a commission for drawing in victims. One way or another, tax scams take advantage of people's greed or their inexperience by offering paybacks and returns that can seem too good to be true. Sometimes, however, they are presented as business opportunities which promise to provide large refunds for smaller investments.

There are many different types of charitable scams that have been used; here are some examples:

- In-kind donation scams

- Charity receipt scams

- Gifting charity scams

- Natural person scams (see section **1.**)

- Business losses scams

- Detaxing scams

The scammers cause an enormous amount of financial damage to their victims. From the costs of participation, to percentages of refunds which must be given back to the scammers, to the CRA's penalties and interest charges, the cost to the victims can be devastating. Besides the devastation done to the victims and their families, sometimes these schemes can tear through an entire workplace, church, or small town.

The case of one particular small town in which I have a number of clients is neither unique nor has it been the subject of television or even local print media. The case is one of a small unknown town in Canada, which like many other small, unknown towns full of honest and hard-working Canadians, has been devastated by a tax scam. The scam that ravaged this small town has helped line the pockets of the scammers with millions of dollars and has left countless of the less than 10,000 residents with enormous tax debts, compounded by years of daily interest and severe penalties.

Many people in this town, unless they are successful at making their case before the CRA or the court, may lose their homes because of the scheme, and many more may lose their retirement savings and their way of life. Because of this particular scheme, and the travelling salesperson who brought this scheme about, this little town has become a different place. There are fewer new cars on the road and fewer family vacations for its residents as well as fewer people who are able to pay for their children's education. This particular little town is a story of how a simple tax scheme which promised the world could ultimately cost the town a large percentage of its capital and savings. It is a story of how a simple tax scheme could affect an entire town's ability to send their children to university and to live the lives they have been working towards.

The story of this particular town and the stories of the churches, workplaces, and extended families where tax schemes have spread like viruses, have helped point to the fact that these schemes run in "trust circles." People get into schemes through those they trust. They inherently trust those in their family. They trust those at their place of worship, and they trust those in their workplace. They also trust their advisors.

When taxpayers see that somebody they trust has legitimately received a large cheque from the government, they too are encouraged to participate and expect to obtain the same result. They trust that they are not being scammed. Their brother, coworker, and church elder would not lead them astray. Why would they? Further, why would their financial advisor or tax preparer lead them astray? When it is a family member, coworker, or a friend, the person usually has nothing to gain and would not intentionally mislead. When it is an advisor who is selling participation in the questionable scheme, it may be through ignorance or perhaps because he or she receives a commission for recruiting taxpayers to participate.

Regardless of who initially introduced the scheme to the taxpayer, and regardless of whether the first wave of participants have received refund cheques from the CRA, taxpayers should be very careful when they consider participating in what may end up being an illegal or unsupported scheme. They should remember that these refund cheques are subject to being clawed back from the taxpayers with interest and penalties.

1. Tax Protesters

One scheme that has various incarnations and which bears numerous names and teachings, involves at its core, tax protesters —individuals who believe or who are led by the scammers to believe that the levying of taxes by the government is either not legitimate, or does not or should not apply to them for some reason.

More often than not, tax protesters believe in some type of the "natural person" theory. Under natural person theories, Canadians have all been enslaved by the government of Canada, or hypothecated to the Pope or some other foreign power in order to pay off a debt from when the country had a secret bankruptcy hundreds of years ago. Part of this enslavement is the issuing of a Social Insurance Number (SIN) by the government, which is used to track Canadian citizens. Generally, these theory teachings are predicated on the understanding that the SIN is its own legal person (or entity) created by the government, and the human attached to the SIN is a separate person — a "natural" person.

The natural person performs the labour in order for the legal person to earn the income, and in turn, the legal person is required to file an income tax return. The natural person is never responsible for paying any income tax or filing any returns.

There are several ways to erase the tax owing through this absurd process. One involves showing that the legal person has not in fact earned any net income through the year. The legal person (i.e., the imaginary legal person which is referred to by the SIN and who is required to file a tax return) earned income, which legal person was required to give to the natural person (i.e., the actual flesh-and-blood person who performed the labour and who requires food and shelter in order to survive). For example, the SIN basically earns $50,000 in the year, but has an expense of $50,000 which it pays to the human so that the human or natural person could pay for his or her living expense. In this scenario, the net income of the legal person is the $50,000 it earned, less the $50,000 it paid out to the natural person. This leaves the legal person with an income of zero, which in turn leaves a tax of zero. In this scam, the labour charge typically appears as "business expenses" on the return of the legal person, and wipes out most or all of the tax owing.

Tax protesters are often heard making the following claims:

- Natural persons are not required to pay income tax under Canadian law. If they were required to, the laws would explicitly say so by providing for natural persons in the legal definition of "persons" under law.

Income tax is not legal and is unconstitutional. It was supposed to be a temporary measure for the war.

Under the *British North America Acts* and the *Magna Carta* income tax is illegal.

They object to paying taxes because some of their taxes are used to fight wars and make weaponry which is against the Convention of Human Rights.

They cannot be convicted of tax evasion because they do not have *mens rea* — they have not done anything wrong.

While there are many schemes used by people to avoid taxes because they are tax protesters, there are a great many people who are not tax protesters, yet become sucked into these schemes, which promise to increase tax refunds. What is common to all these schemes, is that they are perpetrated by fast-talking, seemingly educated, individuals who educate the public on the fact that they should not be paying tax — or should not be paying nearly as much tax as they have been.

These individuals indoctrinate their victims. They charge a fee for the information or for preparing the taxpayer's tax return and they charge a percentage of the return once it arrives. They slip fake business expenses into the return and voila! The taxpayers get a larger refund and pay them their share. Years later, when the CRA discovers what happened the taxpayers are reassessed and charged interest and hefty penalties. They lose their up-front fee and the percentage of the return they gave to the scammer, plus they have to pay penalties and interest, which accumulates each day.

Even if you believe that the government is illegitimately charging you taxes, don't participate in a natural person or other tax protestor scheme. It will just hurt you in the long run. Just because you have or somebody you know has already received a refund, there is no reason why it will not be reassessed as a result of an investigation into such a scheme.

16
FIRST NATIONS TAXATION

The Canadian constitution defines the "Aboriginal peoples of Canada" as including Indian, Inuit, and Métis people, and the *Indian Act* defines who is a Status Indian. It is the *Indian Act* which can have tax consequences, and thus its definition is more relevant fiscally. The act governs much of the relationship between the "registered Indians," their bands, and their reserves, and divides them into two categories: Status and Non-Status.

Status Indians qualify for registration, which means they are entitled to certain rights and payments that will depend on the terms of their particular treaty. Various different treaties allow for things such as payments, hunting and fishing rights, tax exemptions, and free education. In order to become registered with Ottawa as a Status Indian, evidence must

be provided which is both recognized by the government and demonstrates membership in a band. Unfortunately for Non-Status Indians — people who oftentimes cannot prove or have lost their status — they do not qualify for the benefits afforded to Status Indians. Although they consider themselves Indians, without sufficient proof the government does not.

While Aboriginal people in Canada are generally taxed similarly to other Canadians, there are key exceptions which come from section 87 of the *Indian Act*. The Supreme Court of Canada has put forth a test to determine whether section 87 can be used to shield personal income from taxation. This test, called the "Connecting Factors Test," goes through a variety of factors to see if there are enough to deem the income tax exempt. These factors include among others:

- The location of the employer.

- The nature, location, and surrounding circumstances of the work performed by the employee.

- Any benefit to the reserve from the work.

- The residence of the employee.

In general, if it can be shown that 90 percent or more of the work was performed on the reserve, the income should be considered tax exempt. This is a claim which I cannot verify. My entire experience is in dealing with the unlucky 10 percent (or more) who are denied the benefit of the exemption. Many of these are high-income earners who are in fields that are not considered by the Canada Revenue Agency (CRA) to be typical. I always argue that even though my clients may not be hunters or fishermen they still deserve to have the law applied fairly and uniformly. Regardless of how much they earn, their income level should not justify the denial of an exemption.

Under 87(1) of the *Indian Act*, notwithstanding any other act of Parliament or any act of the legislature of a province, but subject to section 83, the following property is exempt from taxation:

- The interest of an Aboriginal or a band in reserve lands or surrendered lands.

- The personal property of an Aboriginal or a band situated on a reserve.

No Aboriginal or band is subject to taxation in respect of the ownership, occupation, possession or use of any property mentioned above or is otherwise subject to taxation in respect of any such property.

1. *Indian Act* Exemption for Employment Income Guidelines

The CRA has put forth a document outlining four guidelines used to determine if income is exempt under section 87 of the *Indian Act*. These four guidelines reproduced in the following sections are not set in stone, and they do not absolutely determine whether income is exempt. It may be entirely possible for income to be exempt, but not fall under these guidelines. The opposite may also be true. The guidelines may indicate that income is exempt, but the CRA may make the contrary finding.

1.1 Guideline 1

When at least 90 percent of the duties of employment are performed on a reserve, all of the income of an Aboriginal from that employment will usually be exempt from income tax.

1.2 Proration rule

When less than 90 percent of the duties of employment are performed on a reserve and the employment income is not exempted by another guideline, the exemption is to be prorated. The exemption will apply to the portion of the income related to the duties performed on the reserve.

1.3 Guideline 2

When the employer is a resident on a reserve and the Aboriginal lives on a reserve, all of the income from the person's employment will usually be exempt from income tax.

1.4 Guideline 3

When more than 50 percent of the duties of an Aboriginal's employment duties are performed on a reserve, and the employer is a resident on a reserve or the Aboriginal lives on a reserve, all of the income from the person's employment will usually be exempt from income tax.

1.5 Guideline 4

When the employer is a resident on a reserve and —

- is an Indian band which has a reserve, or a tribal council representing one or more Indian bands which have reserves;

- is an Indian organization controlled by one or more such bands or tribal councils — if the organization is dedicated exclusively to the social, cultural, educational, or economic development of Aboriginals who for the most part live on reserves; or

- the duties of the employment are in connection with the employer's non-commercial activities carried on exclusively for the benefit of Aboriginals who, for the most part, live on reserves, then all of the income from the person's employment will usually be exempt from income tax.

2. GST and HST

Another consequence of being on the reserve is that GST or HST is not generally applicable on sales made to Status Indians on the reserve, or off-reserve as long as they take the goods to the reserve or have them delivered there after purchase. In order to avoid paying GST or HST while off the reserve, Status Indians are required to produce proof of their status for the merchant.

3. First Nations Self-Taxation

Just because a Status Indian who lives and works on the reserve may not be able to be taxed by the CRA, it does not mean that he or she is immune to taxation.

Section 83 of the *Indian Act* provides — subject to the review of the Indian Taxation Advisory Board and approval by the Minister of Indian Affairs and Northern Development — that band councils may make bylaws for certain purposes including imposing taxes on the use of reserve property.

As permitted under section 83 of the *Indian Act*, by the *First Nations Fiscal and Statistical Management Act* (FSMA), and by the *First Nations Goods and Services Tax Act*, many bylaws have been enacted which impose various types of tax on reserves. These have included property tax, sales tax, and income tax. While these bylaws are binding and have the force of law within a reserve, all federal and provincial laws supersede these bylaws if there is a conflict. However, absent a conflict, all the laws and bylaws work in parallel.

3.1 Property tax

The *Indian Act* provides the ability for *Indian Act* bands to enact bylaws for the taxation of land or interest in land. Similarly, the *First Nations Fiscal and Statistical Management Act* (FSMA) provides similar powers. As one can imagine, having the ability to raise money this way is very attractive, with numerous bands having already established such taxes.

According to Aboriginal Affairs and Northern Development Canada, to date bylaws have been enacted by 134 First Nations under the *Indian Act*, with another 60 bands under FSMA, and in 2010 to 2011, these 194 groups have generated more than $70 million in property taxes.

3.2 First Nations sales tax

This tax which is the same amount as the GST, is imposed by bylaw and levied only by *Indian Act* bands, and applies to sales of fuel, alcohol, and tobacco on the reserve.

Like the provincial tax in all provinces except Quebec, the CRA acts on behalf of the bands to collect and administer the tax, and enforce the relevant bylaws.

According to Aboriginal Affairs and Northern Development Canada, more than $6 million per year is being generated by bands having implemented this tax, which as of November 2011, was a total of eight bands.

3.3 First Nations goods and services tax

This tax, levied by *Indian Act* bands and Aboriginal self-governments, is similar to the First Nations Sales Tax, but is applied on goods and services. It operates just like the GST. Like the First Nations Sales Tax, it is the same amount as the GST and it is administered by the CRA. Further, it replaces the GST where applied.

According to Aboriginal Affairs and Northern Development Canada, more than $12 million per year is being generated by this tax, which as of November 2011, was a total of 23 Aboriginal governments.

3.4 First Nations personal income tax

Levied only by Aboriginal self-governments, this tax acts similar to the income tax system most Canadians are familiar with. There are numerous revenue-sharing programs in which Aboriginal governments may share taxes with provincial and territorial governments.

According to Aboriginal Affairs and Northern Development Canada, this tax currently is the source of $13 million per year to 12 Aboriginal governments.

3.5 Provincial-type taxes

A 2006 amendment to the *First Nations Goods and Services Tax Act* (part 2) makes it possible for certain *Indian Act* bands to impose direct taxes similar to provincial taxes. Such direct taxes include tobacco taxes, liquor consumption taxes, and personal income taxes which may be imposed by the band on people who are in their territory. In order to be permitted to impose such direct taxes, a band must be specifically listed in Schedule 2 of the *First Nations Goods and Services Tax Act*, and the province, also listed in Schedule 2, must agree to the tax.

Indian Act bands or Aboriginal self-governments have already made such arrangements in the Yukon Territory (personal income tax), Saskatchewan (liquor consumption tax), Newfoundland and Labrador (personal income tax and HST revenue sharing), Manitoba (tobacco tax), and British Columbia (tobacco tax). Sometimes this tax appears instead of the provincial equivalent. Other times this tax applies only to Status Indians while the regular provincial tax is applied to all other consumers, both of whom end up paying the same amount of tax.

17
WHEN YOU NEED A LITTLE HELP

Oftentimes, for a variety of reasons, taxpayers get to the point where they need some external help. Sometimes they need an expert who can provide them with options and guide them in the right direction. Other times they need an advocate to stand between them and the Canada Revenue Agency (CRA). Sometimes they need both.

Taxpayers have a variety of options in terms of where they can get help. Help is available from accountants, tax lawyers, the Taxpayers' Ombudsman, and even a taxpayer's Member of Parliament. An accountant may be an inexpensive and quick way to solve various problems, such as a call or letter from the CRA asking for filings. If the filings can be done by the deadline, an accountant is a great way to go. However, if the call or letter threatens legal action, it's best that it is handled by a tax lawyer who can possibly prevent such action, or

defend against the CRA's legal action if it has already started.

1. Taxpayers' Ombudsman

The Taxpayers' Ombudsman is an independent and impartial official who has been appointed to act as an advocate for taxpayers, and is charged with investigation of complaints where taxpayers claim that their rights were breached.

Taxpayers do not approach the ombudsman with help in dealing with an aggressive collector, or in order to help the taxpayers negotiate a payment plan, or to have their bank account unfrozen. The ombudsman does not help negotiate the lifting of a lien — especially if the collections action was taken in a fair and professional manner. The ombudsman does not usually delve into the nitty-gritty subject matter of personal taxes. He or she doesn't look to see if the taxpayer's receipts add up. The ombudsman is looking at a much bigger picture.

Part and parcel with the Taxpayer Bill of Rights, the ombudsman has been appointed to investigate cases where a taxpayer believes that his or her rights have been or are being violated, and report findings to the Minister of National Revenue. If a taxpayer believes that the CRA was being unfair or unprofessional through the process, the ombudsman will investigate to determine whether the taxpayer has been the victim of such unfairness. In such cases where the harsh collections actions are the result of such unfairness, bank accounts may be unfrozen, and collections actions may be dialed-back. However, this is only true when the actions of the CRA were not fair and justified under the circumstances.

The real purposes of the ombudsman is "to assist, advise, and inform the Minister about any matter relating to services provided to a taxpayer by the [CRA]." The ombudsman's mandate is not to help Joe or Sally Taxpayer get a better deal or to be granted taxpayer relief. The ombudsman's role is to fulfill his or her mandate by upholding taxpayer "service rights" from the Taxpayer Bill of Rights, namely:

- Article 5: The right to be treated professionally, courteously, and fairly.
- Article 6: The right to complete, accurate, clear, and timely information from the CRA.
- Article 9: The right to lodge a service complaint and to be provided with an explanation of the CRA findings.
- Article 10: The right to have the costs of compliance taken into account when tax legislation is administered.

- Article 11: The right to expect the CRA to be accountable.
- Article 13: The right to expect the CRA to publish service standards and report annually.
- Article 14: The right to expect the CRA to warn you about questionable tax schemes in a timely manner.
- Article 15: The right to be represented by a person of your choice.

Sometimes through upholding these service rights, the ombudsman does help solve certain problems between a taxpayer and the CRA — especially problems related to the operation of the system itself. A major downfall to asking for help from the ombudsman is that if the taxpayer is simultaneously trying to get help from within the CRA, and the CRA staff know that the ombudsman is involved, I have seen CRA staff all too often, play the "pass-the-buck" game and avoid taking any action on a file until the ombudsman has finished.

1.1 Complaint process

The Taxpayers' Ombudsman provides helpful information on its website (www.oto-boc. gc.ca), where you can also find the complaint form.

As noted on the ombudsman's website, the complaints that can be reviewed are service-related complaints:

- Mistakes that refer to misunderstandings, omissions, or oversights
- Undue delays
- Poor or misleading information
- Unfair treatment
- Staff behaviour

The complaint process consists of four steps:

1. **Acknowledgment:** Once the complaint is prepared and submitted, the ombudsman will acknowledge receipt of the complaint.

2. **Screening:** The ombudsman determines whether the taxpayer has exhausted all the channels within the CRA, and whether the complaint is within the ombudsman's mandate. If not, the complaint is closed and the taxpayer is informed.

3. **Review process:** An examination officer is assigned to the case to review the complaint in a fair and an impartial manner.

4. **Conclusion:** The complaint process ends with the conclusion at which time the ombudsman provides the taxpayer with the outcome of the review as well as any recommendations to the CRA to help resolve the case.

2. The Authorized Representative

There are many reasons why taxpayers may choose to engage a representative to act on their behalf. Experience and understanding of the system are two very important reasons to consider.

Since most taxpayers are not very knowledgeable with respect to tax law or the CRA, they choose to have a representative act on their behalf. This can be anybody they choose including an accountant, a tax lawyer, or even a cousin who is the manager of a shoe store, but who also prepares tax returns every spring! Some choose an accountant for the preparation of their returns and for auditing their company, but they may also choose a tax lawyer for their disputes with the CRA. Taxpayers can empower more than one individual to be an authorized representative.

Sometimes taxpayers engage the services of a representative simply because they are fed up with constantly having to deal with a collections officer who just keeps getting worse and worse, and other times taxpayers choose to find a representative only when bank accounts have become frozen, or once they find out that their entire client list has received a letter advising them to pay all future payables directly to the CRA. Every taxpayer has their own threshold before they choose to ask for help.

The process of designating an authorized representative is easy. Since all taxpayers' information is confidential, the CRA will not be able to release it or discuss it with a representative without the necessary authorization allowing it to do so. For individual taxpayers, they simply have to complete the Authorizing or Cancelling a Representative (T1013) form (see Sample 8) in order to provide such authorization.

2.1 Authorizing a business representative

For businesses, or GST accounts belonging to sole proprietors, all that needs to be done in order to authorize a representative is to complete the Business Consent (RC59) authorization form (see Sample 9), which instead of a Social Insurance Number (required for the personal authorization form), it requires a Business Number (BN).

Since taxpayers may wish to have various different representatives for different purposes, they may choose to limit certain representatives to "level 1" access, where they are not able to make any changes to the taxpayers' accounts, while other representatives may have "level 2" access, allowing changes to be made.

Similarly, an expiry date is provided on the RC59 form, and can be used to limit the amount of time a representative may act. For example, in the course of filing an income tax return, oftentimes tax return preparers include an RC59 or Authorizing or Cancelling a Representative (T1013) form for the client to sign. This enables the tax preparers to file the return, but without an expiry date, they may have the ability to make changes to a taxpayer's account indefinitely.

In order to keep track of a taxpayer's representatives, a business taxpayer may log into "My Business Account" on the CRA's website, where a list of all representatives as well as recent account activity is provided. While online, taxpayers may also authorize further representatives or remove the authority of current ones.

SAMPLE 8
AUTHORIZING OR CANCELLING A REPRESENTATIVE

Canada Revenue Agency   **Agence du revenu du Canada**

Authorizing or Cancelling a Representative

Complete this form to give the Canada Revenue Agency (CRA) your consent to deal with another person (such as your spouse or common-law partner, other family member, friend, or accountant) who would act as your representative for income tax matters or to cancel any existing representatives on your file. Send your completed form to your CRA tax centre. You can find the address of your tax centre on the attached information sheet. To **immediately cancel** a consent, call us at **1-800-959-8281**. You can also give or cancel a consent by providing the requested information online through "Authorize my representative" on our Web site at **www.cra.gc.ca/myaccount**.

Note

We will accept a change of address only from **you** or **your legal representative**. If you have recently moved, call us at **1-800-959-8281** before submitting this form to ensure we have your current mailing address. If you have registered with the **My Account** service, you can change your address by going to **www.cra.gc.ca/myaccount**.

To **authorize** a representative, complete Part 1, Part 2 **or** Part 3, Part 4, and Part 6.

To **cancel** a representative, complete Part 1, Part 5, and Part 6.

Part 1 – Taxpayer information

Complete this part to identify yourself and to give your account number.
You will need to complete a **separate Form T1013** for each account.

First name	Last name	Work telephone number	Home telephone number
John	Doe	416 – 555-5555	–

	Individual	Trust	T5
Complete the one that applies:	Social insurance number 1 2 3 4 5 6 7 8 9	Trust account number T	T5 filer identification number H A

To authorize your representative for online access, complete Part 2; otherwise, complete Part 3.

Part 2 – Giving consent for a representative (including online access)

You must complete a separate Form T1013 for each representative. Note that online access is not available for trust accounts. Please fill out Part 3 of the form to give your consent to a representative for your trust account.

To grant online access to your representative, enter his or her identification number.

For an individual
RepID

or

For a group
GroupID
G

or

For a business
Business Number (BN)

Your representative must have registered the BN with the CRA **"Represent a Client"** service.

Enter the full name of the individual, group or business.

Name of individual associated to the RepID

First name: Last name:

Name of the group associated to the GroupID

Name of the business associated to the BN

Enter the **level of authorization** (level 1 or 2):

If you **do not specify a level** of authorization, we will **assign a level 1**.

Our online services do not have a year-specific option. Therefore, your representative will have access to **all tax years**.

Part 3 – Giving consent for a representative (other than online access)

You must complete a separate Form T1013 for each representative.
- If you are giving consent for an **individual**, enter the individual's full name in the appropriate box below.
- If you are giving consent for a **business**, enter the name of the business in the appropriate box below.

Name of individual

First name:

Last name:

Name of business

Telephone: –   –   Ext: Fax: –   –

Part 3 continued on the next page ➜

T1013 E (11)   (Vous pouvez obtenir ce formulaire en français à www.arc.gc.ca ou au 1-800-959-3376.)   **Canada**

Part 3 (Continued)

Tick either:

- **Box A** below to give consent for **all tax years and** specify the level of authorization; **or**
- **Box B** below to give consent for a **specific** tax year or years **and** specify the level of authorization for **each** tax year.

If you **do not specify a level** of authorization, we will **assign a level 1**.

☐   **A.** All (past, present, and future) tax years   **Level of authorization** (level 1 or 2): ☐

☐   **B.** Enter the applicable tax year or years (past and/or present), and specify the level of authorization (level 1 or 2) for **each** tax year.

Tax year(s)									
Level of authorization									

Month   Day

If this consent is for a **trust account** and the year-end is not December 31, enter the month and day of the year-end. ☐☐☐☐

Part 4 – Consent expiry date

Enter an expiry date for the consent given in **Part 2** or **Part 3** if you want the consent to end at a particular time. Your consent will stay in effect until **you** or **your representative** cancels it, it reaches the expiry date you choose, or we are notified of your death.

Year   Month   Day

Part 5 – Cancelling one or more existing consents

Complete this section **only** to cancel an existing consent. Tick the appropriate box.

☐   **A.** Cancel **all** consents.   ☐   **B.** Cancel the consents given for the individual, group or business identified below:

Name of individual   **Name of business**

First name: Last name:

RepID	**or**	GroupID	**or**	Business Number
		G		

Part 6 – Signature

You or **your legal representative** (for example, a person with your power of attorney, your guardian, or an executor or administrator of the taxpayer's estate) must sign and date this form. If you are signing and dating this form as the legal representative, tick the box below. If two or more legal representatives are acting jointly on the taxpayer's behalf, the signature of each legal representative is required. Also, send us a copy of the legal document that identifies you as the legal representative, if you have not already done so.

By signing and dating this form, you authorize us to deal with the individual, group, or business identified in **Part 2** or **Part 3** and/or to cancel the consents shown in **Part 5**.

We will not process this form unless it is **signed and dated** by you or your legal representative.
This form must be received by the CRA **within six months** of its signature date. If not, it will not be processed.

☐   **I am not the taxpayer named in part 1 of this form.** However, I have power of attorney for this taxpayer, I am the legal guardian of this taxpayer, or I am the executor/administrator of this taxpayer's estate.

John Doe
Print name of taxpayer or each legal representative

x   _Doe_
Signature of taxpayer or each legal representative

Year   Month   Day
2 0 1 2 0 6 1 1
Date of signature

Privacy Act, Personal Information Bank numbers CRA PPU 005 and CRA PPU 175

BARCODE

SAMPLE 9
BUSINESS CONSENT FORM

Business Consent form

Complete this form to consent to the release of confidential information about your program account(s) to the representative named below, or to cancel consent for an existing representative. **Send this completed form to your tax centre (see Instructions).** Make sure you complete this form correctly, since we cannot change the information that you provided. You can also give **or** cancel consent by providing the requested information online through My Business Account at **www.cra.gc.ca/mybusinessaccount**.
Note: Read all the instructions on the first page before completing this form.

Part 1 – Business information – Complete this part to identify your business (all fields have to be completed)

Business name: *ABC Corp.*   BN: |0|1|2|3|4|5|6|7|8|

Telephone number: *416·444·4444*

Part 2 – Authorize a representative – Complete either part a) or b)

a) Authorize access by telephone, fax, mail or in person by appointment

If you are giving consent for an individual, enter that person's full name. If you are giving consent to a firm, enter the name and BN of the firm. If you want us to deal with a specific individual in that firm, enter **both** the individual's name and the firm's name and BN. If you do not identify an individual of the firm, then you are giving us consent to deal with anyone from that firm.

Note: If you are authorizing a representative (individual or firm) who is not registered with the "Represent a Client" service, the phone number is required.

Name of Individual: _____   Name of Firm: _____

Telephone number: _____   BN: | | | | | | | | | |

or

b) Authorize online access (includes access by telephone, fax, mail or by appointment)

You can authorize your representative to deal with us through our online service for representatives. The BN must be registered with the "Represent a Client" service to be an online representative. **Our online service does not have a year-specific option, so your representative will have access to all years.** Please enter the name and RepID of the individual or the name of the group and GroupID **or** name and BN of the firm.

Name of individual: _____   **and**   RepID: | | | | | | | |
or
Name of group: _____   **and**   GroupID: |G| | | | | |
or
Name of firm: _____   **and**   BN: | | | | | | | | | |

Telephone number: _____

Part 3 – Select the program accounts, years and authorization level

a) Program Accounts – Select the program accounts the above individual or firm is authorized to access (tick only box A **or** B).

A. ☐   This authorization applies to all program accounts and all years.

Expiry date: | | | | | | | | |

and

Authorization level (tick level 1 or 2)

☐ Level 1 lets CRA disclose information only on your program account(s);   **or**

☐ Level 2 lets CRA disclose information **and** accept changes to your program account(s).

or

B. ☐   This authorization applies only to program accounts and periods listed in Part 3b). If you ticked this option, you must complete 3b).

RC59 E (11)   Page 1 of 2

Business Consent form

b) Details of program accounts and fiscal periods – Complete this area only if you ticked box B in Part 3a) on page 1.

If you ticked box B in part 3a), you have to provide at least one program identifier (see Instructions on page 1). You can then tick the box "All program accounts" for that program identifier **or** enter a reference number. Provide the authorization level (tick **either** box 1 to allow the CRA to disclose information **or** box 2 to disclose information **and** accept changes to your program account).

You can also tick the box "All years" to allow unlimited tax year access **or** enter a specific fiscal period (specific period authorization **is not available** for online access). You can also enter an expiry date to automatically cancel authorization. If more authorizations or more than four program identifiers are needed, complete another Form RC59.

Program identifier	All program accounts	Reference number	Authorization level		All years	or	Specific fiscal period (not available for online access)	Expiry date
			1	2			Year-end	
☐☐	☐ or	☐☐☐☐	☐	☐	☐	or	‖‖‖‖‖‖‖	‖‖‖‖‖‖‖
☐☐	☐ or	☐☐☐☐	☐	☐	☐	or	‖‖‖‖‖‖‖	‖‖‖‖‖‖‖
☐☐	☐ or	☐☐☐☐	☐	☐	☐	or	‖‖‖‖‖‖‖	‖‖‖‖‖‖‖
☐☐	☐ or	☐☐☐☐	☐	☐	☐	or	‖‖‖‖‖‖‖	‖‖‖‖‖‖‖

Part 4 – Cancel one or more authorizations – Complete this part **only** to cancel authorization(s)

A. ☐ Cancel **all** authorizations.

B. ☐ Cancel authorization for the individual, group, or firm identified below.

C. ☐ Cancel authorization for specific program account(s) _____

Name of individual: _____ and RepID: ☐☐☐☐☐☐☐
    or
Name of group: _____ and GroupID: G ☐☐☐☐☐
    or
Name of firm: _____ and BN: ☐☐☐☐☐☐☐☐☐
Telephone number: _____

Part 5 – Certification

This form has to be signed by an authorized person of the business such as an owner, a partner of a partnership, a director of a corporation, an officer of a non-profit organization or a trustee of an estate.
By signing and dating this form, you authorize the CRA to deal with the individual, group, or firm listed in Part 2 of this form or cancel the authorizations listed in Part 4.

First name: _John_   Last name: _Doe_

Sign here: ▶ _Doe_   Date: |2|0|Y|2|0|6|1|1|

This form will not be processed unless it is signed and dated by an authorized person of the business.

Privacy Act, Personal Information Bank numbers CRA PPU 175 and CRA PPU 223

Page 2 of 2

CONCLUSION

You may choose to think of the Canada Revenue Agency (CRA) as a long river which most taxpayers sail up and down without any problems whatsoever. Those who have little or no interaction with the CRA are on smooth water. The weather is fine, the sun is out, and they have a great ride along the water. However, some of these taxpayers simply lose their way and start to head towards turbulent waters. Sometimes they were not paying attention, and other times they are simply pushing the limits of their boat. These taxpayers need a little guidance and often just require a simple point in the right direction so they can head back to calmer waters. For these taxpayers, perhaps this book has helped do just that. For those taxpayers who are deep into turbulent waters and are heading over the rapids towards the waterfall downstream, it is sometimes best to abandon the "do-it-yourself" approach. Hiring an expert to navigate their boat back from the brink while they stand dry and observe from the shore may be their best option. Most importantly, when these taxpayers are navigating down the river and they see the police waving guns and badges from the shore, it is always best to have a tax lawyer on their side.

The CRA is given a tremendous amount of power to do its job, and standing behind this power are the courts, police, and prisons which can enforce compliance. However, the taxpayer is not without a voice. The Charter of Rights and Freedoms offers protection to taxpayers being investigated criminally, which includes the right against self-incrimination and the right against unreasonable search and seizure. While sometimes difficult to uphold, the Taxpayer Bill of Rights guarantees a number of rights, of which the Taxpayers' Ombudsman will help uphold the service-related ones. At the end of the day, when taxpayers need help, tax lawyers are available to help the taxpayers through the turbulent water.

The best way to not need this help is to always do the right thing. File honestly, correctly, and on time. Pay on time. Don't participate in tax schemes, and always have all of the necessary paperwork to justify your expense claims. If you play your cards right and you are diligent, you too may survive the CRA.